Sing O Barren

LISA HARRIS-CORBITT

A Word from The Author

As you read my deeply personal story, you will wonder why I had to suffer so much pain, abuse, shame, abandonment and rejection. You may even question God as to why He allowed this to happen to me. I went through this for you, or someone you know who endured the same experiences that I have, so that God could use me to minister healing and deliverance to you. I believe that it is only when you have had the same experiences as someone else that you will be able to effectively help them.

Women, both young and old, and men (Yes! Men!) who have read my book have all received healing while reading it. I am every woman in this book. There is something for every woman to identify with in my book. Every woman who reads of my experiences has said "That's me!" to one, some or all of them.

There is a healing anointing and impartation that takes place when you read Sing O Barren. But you must first open up your heart and receive God's healing. God loves you no matter what you have done or what's been done to you. Please contact me and let me know how this book has brought healing to you. My contact information is at the end of the book.

    I love you and want you to be healed and delivered.

                  Lisa A Corbitt

Sing o Barren is a powerful and gripping memoir of unbelievable trials, intense personal pain yet also one of incredible favor and triumph. I couldn't put this book down until the last page was turned. A gripping read. This intensely deep and personal look into the early life of this incredible yet humble servant of God challenged me to take God at His every word. I'm not insignificant, I'm not a nobody and neither are you. In your pain there is hope. God can use your story for His glory. Don't give up, only give it to Jesus.

-Charisse Broome, Author, "Thank You Abba"

I personally have been touched by this book because it really showed me how God can deliver anyone despite great difficulties they face in life. From the moment I began reading this book I could not stop because it was very intense and real and the more I read was the more I wanted to read. The book also opened my eyes to things I was never aware of before. Sing O Barren is a book that will save people's lives. *–Hernamia Salcedo , Psychology Professional*

I could not put down this book until I read it to the end. My eyes were riveted to Lisa Corbitt's personal story of overcoming abuse.
Sing O Barren is not just another story of abuse. It an extremely inspirational book, orchestrated by God, and based on Lisa's experiences, which demonstrates the power of God to heal a broken life and to give beauty for ashes. You will receive healing and deliverance when you read this book. *-Carole Bridgeman, Pastor*

Sing O Barren

Copyright © 2017 Lisa Harris-Corbitt
All rights reserved.
ISBN: 978-0-9893357-7-5

GOSPEL INKS BOOKS
www.gospelinks.com

Sing O Barren

ISBN: 978-0-9893357-7-5

Library of Congress Control Number: 2017902998

Copyright © 2017 by Lisa Harris-Corbitt

All rights reserved. No part of this book may be reproduced or transmitted in any form or by any means without written permission from the publisher.

Some names in this book have been changed to protect the privacy of those involved in the events depicted.

Unless otherwise noted, all Scripture quotations are from the New King James Version of the Bible. Copyright © 1982 by Thomas Nelson, Inc. Used by permission. All rights reserved.

Published by Gospel Inks
www.gospelinks.com
407-878-0298

Cover Photo by Danielle Marroquin- www.unsplash.com
Cover Design by Gospel Inks

Printed in the United States of America
Revised February 2017

Dedication

This book is dedicated to my Lord and Savior Jesus Christ, whose sacrifice on the Cross has given me abundant and eternal life, and to my Heavenly Father who loves me and has rescued me from death. I also dedicate this book to the Holy Spirit who is my comforter and friend.

Acknowledgments

I thank my sister and my brother for their love and support.

To my sister-in-law -thank you for the healing and deliverance that you brought to my life.

Thank you, my dear friend, Judith Marshall for your wonderful friendship and support.

I thank my cousin Diana Mollon, her husband David Mollon and their family for all the help and support they have always given to me, and for rescuing me on many occasions.

I also thank Pastor Earland Banfield and his wife Jennifer whose ministry and lives have powerfully impacted and transformed my life.

I also thank everyone who the Lord has used along my painful journey to support me and minister healing and deliverance to me.

delivering me, healing me, saving me and loving me.

"Sing, O Barren. You who have not borne! Break forth into singing, and cry aloud, You who have not labored with child! For more are the children of the desolate than the children of the married woman" says the LORD.

"Enlarge the place of your tent, and let them stretch out the curtains of your dwellings; Do not spare; lengthen your cords, and strengthen your stakes. For you shall expand to the right and to the left, And your descendants will inherit the nations, And make the desolate cities inhabited.

"Do not fear, for you will not be ashamed; Neither be disgraced, for you will not be put to shame; For you will forget the shame of your youth, And will not remember the reproach of your widowhood anymore. For your Maker is your husband. The LORD of hosts is His name; And your Redeemer is the Holy One of Israel; He is called the God of the whole earth.

For the LORD has called you: Like a woman forsaken and grieved in spirit, Like a youthful wife when you were refused"

Isaiah 54: 1-6

Contents

Chapter 1	Birth Day: Birth Trauma	12
Chapter 2	Skeletons In The Closet	16
Chapter 3	Faulty Foundations	22
Chapter 4	Battered Child	30
Chapter 5	Running away From Home	34
Chapter 6	Please Don't Kill the Kittens	37
Chapter 7	Memorable Moments	44
Chapter 8	Why Daddy Why?	50
Chapter 9	Looking For Love In All The Wrong Places	63
Chapter 10	Stalked......and Beaten	72
Chapter 11	Please Let Me Die	80
Chapter 12	Moving to America	91
Chapter 13	Pregnant.......and Beaten	96
Chapter 14	Et tu Uncle Simon?	101
Chapter 15	Finding God's Love In The Midst of Abuse and Brokenness	106
Chapter 16	The Sins of My Father	113
Chapter 17	Still........The Depression	116

Chapter 18	Mommy Do You Love Me?	120
Chapter 19	Early Encounters With God	128
Chapter 20	Miracles From Heaven	132
Chapter 21	The Presence of God	136
Chapter 22	Deliver Me From Evil	142
Chapter 23	Back in The Fire	150
Chapter 24	Battered Wife	156
Chapter 25	Back to Williamsville	165
Chapter 26	More Abuse	169
Chapter 27	"If You Leave Me You Will Die"	174
Chapter 28	Escape	180
Chapter 29	Learning To Live, Laugh & Love Myself	187
Chapter 30	Death, Death and More Death	192
Chapter 31	The Barren Now "Sings"	196

Chapter 1
Birth Day: Birth Trauma

My life began dramatically on the Caribbean island of Trinidad on a sun drenched Sunday afternoon in 1956. Unlike my siblings, the events surrounding my birth were very traumatic. On the day of my birth alone, I had three near death experiences resulting in birth trauma. Statistically, most babies who experience birth trauma develop severe psychological, emotional and physical problems throughout part or most of their lives. Such was the case with me. This trend would continue in my life all the way into adulthood........until I learned to "sing" in spite of the barrenness in my life.

My parents, Harold and Yvonne Harris, married in 1949 and later had a son and a daughter, the perfect family, and therefore did not want to have any more children. But my mother became pregnant with me anyway. So along I came, unplanned by my parents, but predestined by God to be born. My mother had a difficult and complicated pregnancy with me and had to be confined to complete bed rest for almost her entire term. One of those complications being, that for the first five months of her pregnancy, Mummy had what appeared to be a normal menstrual cycle. Her gynecologist determined that she would have to have a Cesarean Section, as it would be impossible for me to be delivered by natural means.

The C section took place on April 22nd. The surgery went well, but as I was plucked from my mother's womb, my entire body was blue. I was not breathing! I had what is commonly known as Blue Baby Syndrome. Blue Baby Syndrome is when a baby appears blue at_birth due to lack of oxygen. Typically, blue babies are born with a congenital heart defect that causes a bluish coloration of the skin as a result of cyanosis. Cyanosis is a severe condition indicating a lack of oxygen in the blood supply. This can arise due to various severe illnesses that inhibit circulation or oxygen.

In those days, medical technology was not advanced as it is now, so the only recourse the doctor had was to slap my buttocks to induce crying which would then force oxygen into my lungs causing me to breathe. He slapped me once, but I did not cry and was still not breathing. He slapped me again and again, but still nothing. In a panic, the doctor grabbed the nearest surgical needle and plunged it into my thigh. Instantly, my screams erupted throughout the operating room and I took my first breath.

Meanwhile, my father was waiting in the balcony outside the operating room completely oblivious to what had taken place inside. The open balcony, which was on the fifth floor of the hospital, was supported by a narrow ledge.

Shortly after the events that took place in the operating room, the door opened and a nurse emerged carrying a small round basin. Suddenly, realizing that she forgot something inside, she placed the basin on the narrow ledge and ran back into the operating room. Two minutes elapsed, then five. Little by little, something inside the basin began to move. The movements began to grow quicker and quicker. Curious to see what was causing this strange phenomenon, my father walked over to the basin and peered inside. There I was, wrapped in a green blanket and squirming. Any move I made could have tipped the basin over and send me plunging over the side to an early death. Daddy scooped me up in his arms hurriedly just as the nurse surfaced once more. He swore at her violently for her carelessness.

Three days after these traumatic episodes, my thigh developed a cavity that became engorged with pus. This horribly painful abscess was caused by the needle which the doctor had frantically stuck into my thigh. The needle, having been previously used, was infected with bacteria and consequently caused me to develop the abscess. I was in excruciating pain and became irritable and cranky. At three days old, the doctor had to surgically remove the abscess from my thigh. It left a scar and a slight dent in my upper left thigh, which I still have to this day.

When I was fully recovered, my parents took me home to join my siblings, Leslie and Alan and my father's mother, Ivy, who lived with us. Our house was large, beautiful and comfortable, but our family was very dysfunctional. This dysfunctionality had its roots in both my mother's and my father's families.

Chapter 2
Skeletons In The Closet

Mummy's father, Edgar Paul, whom we affectionately called Granddaddy, was of African descent. His parents, Albert and Catherine Paul, migrated from Africa to Trinidad in the early 1900s. They brought with them their African customs and religion and continued to practice them in Trinidad. Their children, who were born in Trinidad, were all branded with tribal marks. Albert and Catherine became devoted Catholics and encouraged their children to embrace their new religion. Granddaddy's siblings practiced their parents' Yoruba religion in addition to Catholicism, but Granddaddy remained a devout Catholic.

Granddaddy was a fine looking man who loved to dance and dress well. He was a strong man with a gentle and loving spirit, and possessed great integrity and character. As a young man, Granddaddy met and fell in love with a young Portuguese woman named Isabella De Peiza whose parents had migrated to Trinidad from Madeira. He was dark skinned and she was light skinned. In those days there was a lot more prejudice, so because of the differences in their skin color there was no little opposition to the union. But love prevailed and they got married.

Grandma Isabella was a born again Christian and a member of the Nazarene Church. She and Granddaddy had five children, two daughters and three sons. When she became pregnant with their sixth child, Grandma Isabella died in childbirth. My mother was only eight years old when she died. Granddaddy never married and raised his children by himself.

Granddaddy did an excellent job of raising his children, but when a female relative fell in love with an older married man and became pregnant, he was devastated. Not desiring the same fate for his younger daughter, he sent my mother to live with his niece Lana where he thought she would escape the same predicament.

Unknown to my grandfather, Lana, her brother Wally, my grandfather's siblings and other family members belonged to the occult. I only discovered this horrible secret when I became an older adult. They held clandestine meetings at Lana's house where they wore white robes and performed secret rituals. They did blood sacrifices and pronounced curses and spells over people. Summarily, they were practicing witchcraft.

Lana tried to recruit my mother into their cult, and compelled her to wear the occult garments they wore. In addition, she cruelly abused my mother. When my grandfather discovered what was happening, he immediately moved my mother back home. Mummy's sister Elaine had already gotten married and now lived with her husband.

Now being the only daughter and sister in a house of five men, my mother became the center of attention which resulted in her becoming self-centered and spoiled. According to family members, my grandfather had a very frustrating time raising my mother. She was headstrong, manipulative, unruly and disobedient.

Not too long after she moved back home, my mother was sexually molested by one of her brothers. She never told anyone about it until a few years before her death.

Daddy was the eldest of three boys. Their father died when Daddy was only nine years old. Daddy's two younger brothers, Clyde and Earl, migrated to America and England respectively when they were teenagers. My father, however, remained in Trinidad and continued to live with his mother in the family home.

After her husband's death and the subsequent migration of her two younger sons, my grandmother became very dependent on my father and very possessive of him. They had a very close and utterly strange relationship. Grand mummy, as we called her, treated my father as though he was her husband and not her son, a relationship probably brought about by the fact that since her husband's death and the migration of her two younger sons, my father became the "man of the house". He was the one that she turned to for comfort and support. He was the one who took care of her. He paid the bills and maintained the house.

Daddy and Mummy met in 1949. He was twenty two and she was twenty three. Daddy was very handsome and liked by many girls. Mummy was pretty and vivacious and Daddy fell for her instantly. They were ardently in love.

Daddy wrote her father asking for his consent to be engaged to my mother for a period of three years culminating in marriage. Not wanting Mummy to engage in premarital sex and become pregnant as their female relative did, my grandfather's written reply to my father was "I am however of the opinion that the period of three years mentioned by you is unduly long having regard to the many temptations that you both would certainly have to encounter during the course of the period mentioned".

Notwithstanding, shortly after their engagement, Mummy became pregnant. In those days pre-marital pregnancy was taboo and scandalous. The only obvious choice for them was to get married. They married in June 1950 and my sister, Leslie was born in December the same year.

When my parents got married, Daddy moved my mother into the house he shared with his mother. Overnight, the strange bond that existed between my grandmother and my father became threatened. To my Grandmother, Mummy was "the other woman". My mother no longer experienced being the center of attraction she enjoyed before she married my father because my father's attention was now consumed by his mother. An intense hatred ensued between my mother and my grandmother. Grandmummy was jealous of Mummy and treated her with absolute disgust because she was her son's wife. My mother hated my grandmother because she was the focus of my father's attention.

And so, they contended violently for Daddy's affection. They argued about everything and agreed on nothing. Grandmummy wanted to continue running the household as she normally did prior to her son's marriage. Mummy felt that she should run the house because after all she was now his wife. Daddy consulted Grandmummy for almost everything and alienated my mother. There was always screaming, cursing and tantrums. It was to this volatile and dysfunctional environment I came after I was born.

When I was born, my father became more devoted to me than my grandmother, my mother and my two siblings. He lavished me with love and attention which made both my mother and grandmother jealous and enraged. They now felt that they were both being spurned by my father. The only thing my grandmother and my mother now agreed on was their hatred of me. Together they reviled and mistreated me and spoke all manner of evil curses over me.

Because behaviors are learned, especially when you are young and impressionable, my brother and sister emulated my mother's open and vocal dislike of me. I was to become the object of contempt, rejection, ridicule and abuse which would have a destructive effect on my life, relationships and choices for many years. When I turned fifty, my siblings and I finally spoke about all that we had endured from our parents. At this writing, we have only now begun to have a real relationship as brother and sisters.

Chapter 3
Faulty Foundations

We were a middle class family. My father had a prominent position with the Trinidad and Tobago Government as a Budget Analyst. He was an intelligent man who, when he was younger, wanted to become a doctor. But financially, his mother could not afford to send him to medical school. Mummy worked as a sales clerk at a major department store in Port of Spain, the country's capital.

My siblings and I were well cared for materially. We wore the best clothes, were well fed, and got an abundance of the latest toys and other gifts at Christmas and on our birthdays. My parents always bought us many books, and from a very young age I loved to read and became fascinated by the stories I read.

Our house, the original family home my father grew up in, was rebuilt not too long after I was born. The new house was large and beautiful. It had many steps leading up to a front porch, a huge living room with a dining room area, three bedrooms and a large kitchen. There was a garage to the side of the house and a large yard in the back. Most of the back yard was paved.

Grandmummy had a kindergarten in the kitchen. As a result, there was always an influx of children in our home. I especially liked that because I always had someone to play with as my siblings and I did not get along well at all. The battle lines were drawn in our family. The opposing sides consisted of Mummy, Mummy against Daddy, Grandmummy against Lisa, Mummy against Lisa, Grandmummy and Mummy against Lisa, Mummy, Leslie and Alan against Lisa, Daddy against Alan, Alan against Lisa, Leslie, Alan and me against each other interchangeably and so on. The sides changed, but the consensus was the same – I was the target because I was my father's 'pet'.

At an incredibly young age, I began to sense that something was terribly wrong with our family. One day, when I was two years old, Daddy and I were home alone. The rest of the family had gone out, and Daddy was designated to stay at home to baby sit me. We were in the kitchen, and Daddy was sitting on one of the school benches watching me play. Slowly, he pulled something out of a bag he was carrying. It was a pair of black panties that he had bought me. He then took off all my clothes, put the black panties on me and then ogled me as I innocently continued to play. Suddenly, his breathing grew harder and harder. I was too young to know it at the time, but he was getting sexually aroused. He then commented, "When you get older, you are going to look so good" I was too young to know at that time that his behavior was inappropriate, but the memory of what he did has stayed with me all my life.

My father was a sexual deviant. Shortly after my parents' wedding, Daddy began to have numerous sexual affairs. This trend would continue during my parents' entire marriage. In the years preceding his death, we would discover that he had many sexual liaisons with prostitutes.

Grandmummy enjoyed seeing Mummy hurt whenever Daddy cheated on her. She was delighted that Daddy was unfaithful to my mother and encouraged his infidelity because of the pain it caused Mummy. When Daddy came home from one of his illicit dates, and the shouting erupted between my parents, Grandmummy was gleeful. My grandmother did everything she could to break up the marriage, treating my mother despicably at every opportunity. But, my mother fought back with her own brand of detestable behavior.

Once, Mummy tried to kill Grand mummy. She grabbed a knife out of the kitchen drawer and pointed it at her menacingly. Grandmummy ran around the kitchen table with Mummy chasing her with the knife, threatening to kill her. Grandmummy was screaming, my father was screaming at my mother, and we, the children, were bawling with fear.

The bickering, fighting, and dysfunctionality in the Harris household affected us, the children the most. We suffered mentally, emotionally and physically. My sister Leslie developed an anxiety disorder. Her heart palpitated frantically and she would think she was having a heart attack. She constantly pressed her hand against her heart to see check if it was still beating. This consistent hand to heart ritual caused all her clothes to become worn out in the chest area.

The anxiety attacks occurred at any time, day or night, but it was more pronounced at night. She would wake up in the middle of the night believing that she was having a heart attack and was going to die. There were many nights that my parents had to take her to the hospital, but the doctors could find nothing physically wrong with her.

My brother suffered with low self-esteem. He was angry all the time. I never knew what would make him erupt. He and Daddy had a very acrimonious relationship. When he became an adult, Daddy told my brother that he hated him since he was born. I suffered with low self-esteem, depression, anxiety attacks, night terrors, irrational fears, suicidal thoughts, and nervous and emotional disorders.

As children and young adults, we all suffered with Tourette's Syndrome, which we inherited from our father. Tourette's syndrome is a neurological illness characterized by repetitive, involuntary movements and vocalizations called tics or spasms. These tics include eye blinking, facial grimacing, the repetitive use of words or phrases, head or shoulder jerking, and repetitive throat clearing, sniffing, and grunting sounds.

Tourette's Syndrome may be caused by emotional and physical problems, stress, and fears about dreadful things happening. People with Tourette's Syndrome also have problems with depression or anxiety disorders. The tics become worse with excitement, anxiety or worry.

I believe that we all developed Tourette's Syndrome because of the stressful atmosphere in the home. In my father's case, he would make strange high pitched vocal noises while jerking his head violently back and forth. Leslie made repetitive hand to chest movements while my brother would thrust his tongue rapidly in and out of his mouth. I would walk a few yards, stoop down and then jump up quickly. I repeated this pattern several times as I walked.

At the age of two, another devastating incident took place which would haunt me for many years. In my native country, Trinidad and Tobago, (Tobago being the smaller island) there is a carnival that takes place each year. Trinidad and Tobago Carnival, which is dubbed "the greatest show on earth," is displayed on the nation's streets in a festival of revelry. People dress in lavishly expensive costumes and dance through the streets in large groups called bands to the beat of the steelpan, brass bands or drums. While 90% of the costumes are modern, many people like to wear traditional costumes from the 1800s when carnival first originated. One of those traditional costumes is called "Jab Molassie". Jab is the French patois for 'Diable' (Devil), and Molassie is the French patois for Mélasse

(Molasses). The costume consists of a pair of swim trunks worn by the men and a skimpy pants and top worn by the women. The Jab Molassie adorn themselves with a wire tail, mask, horns on their heads and a pitchfork in their hands.

These costumed bands of Jab Molassie usually carry chains, and wear locks and keys around their waist. Their entire bodies are smeared with either grease, mud, black, red, blue or white paint. They gyrate to a rhythmic mesmerizing beat that is played on tin pans. While gyrating, they thrust their pitchforks in a sinister way at people. In the pursuit of fun and merriment, the goal of the Jab Molassie is to terrify people. The entire performance is paganish and diabolically petrifying.

When I was two years old, a band of Jab Molassie ran into our house to frighten us. I was playing alone in the living room at the time when they slammed open the front gate and ran through our house. They beat their tin cans ominously as they thrust their pitchforks back and forth in supposed "fun". I screamed and my parents came running. I instantly became ill.

The grisly experience plunged me into an abyss of fear which lasted for many, many years until I was delivered by the power of God. Out of that experience emerged a hatred of Carnival and anything evil. Each year, whenever Carnival came around and the preparations and pre-carnival shows were taking place, I grew horribly ill. I developed a high fever, loss of appetite and lost at least ten pounds. I became almost catatonic as the spirit of fear gripped me. My parents would take the entire family to watch the Carnival parade which takes place all day on the Monday and Tuesday preceding Ash Wednesday. We sat in the Stands to look at the masqueraders dancing to the rhythmically infectious beat of the steelpans and the brass bands. While everyone enjoyed the endless parade, I lay on the seat - sick, feverish and glassy eyed - terrified to look at the spectacle.

The whole experience was utterly horrifying to me. I began suffering with night terrors. I used to have a recurring nightmare where I was standing in the street in front of our house. Suddenly a band of Jab Molassie would run down the street to come and kill me. I would try to run, but my feet would be permanently glued to the ground. I often woke up screaming, drenched in sweat and breathing fast.

It did not matter how sick or terrified I was. Each year, my parents would still take me to see the Carnival. No amount of pleading and begging them to leave me at my aunt's house would move them.

When I was eight years old, a dreadful experience similar to the one I had when I was two occurred again. This time, my sister and brother were leaning over our front fence talking to some friends. Suddenly one of our friends saw a Jab Molassie band passing on the main road at the top of our street. They yelled at them to come down our street. Suddenly, the Jab Molassie band changed directions and ran down our street.

My siblings and I ran screaming into the house and hid under our parents' bed while our friends laughed raucously. We were not amused.

Chapter 4
Battered Child

My mother highly favored my sister and brother, but hated me. She showered them with affection and treated them well, but me she abused verbally, emotionally and physically. She hated me and so did my grandmother. Mummy constantly told me "You are so stupid". "Why can't you be like your sister?' "You will never amount to anything". "You will never get married". "No one will ever want you." "You can't do anything right". "You are a failure". "You will never succeed at anything" All those slurs she spoke to me were word curses that would have a catastrophic effect over me almost all my life.

A word curse is a negative word spoken over a person that has the power to make the thing spoken be fulfilled. Examples of word curses are "You are a fool" "You will get pregnant at 14 like your mother did" "All the women in my family die when they are 27, so I will die too". The Bible warns about the danger of speaking death over people. In the book of Proverbs, Chapter 18 and verse 21 it says "Death and life are in the power of the tongue, and those who love it will eat its fruit." Our words are powerful and have the capacity to produce life or death. When someone tells you "You can never do anything right", it can become a self-fulfilling prophecy, that is, it can cause the thing said to be fulfilled.

I was blamed for everything bad that happened. I was blamed so often that I believed that I was to blame for everything that went wrong and often confessed to things I did not do. I took this belief into my adulthood. I blamed myself for everything that anyone did or said, and I experienced feelings of extreme guilt and worthlessness. I am in no way implying that I was perfect. I was like any other child, sometimes mischievous, eating unhealthy food without permission or not listening to my parents. But I was never the horrible child my mother said I was.

I was a very precocious child. I had a witty answer for any comment or question leveled at me. I was curious about everything and everyone and asked a lot of questions. That was one of the ways I gained knowledge about various subjects. I was also a tomboy and played more with the neighborhood boys than the girls.

Everything I did or said, good and not so good, annoyed my mother all her life. Mummy seemed to make it her life's mission to insult me, ridicule me and spurn me. I did everything I knew to make her love me and treat me well, but she never did. Mummy never hugged me, and only told me she loved me, once, a couple years before she died.

She punished me for everything. She would beat me badly with a thick leather belt. Any time I saw her with the belt I would tremble violently. Once, I was riding my bike up and down our street. My parents always told me and my siblings that we were only to ride our bikes on our street. But this particular day when I rode my bike to the top of our street, I ventured into the adjacent street to turn my bike around and ride back down our street. By the time I rode back to our house, my mother was waiting for me with the belt and beat me severely.

Sometimes Mummy would beat me in the head with the broom handle. I remember one such incident when I was seven years old. Every few months, on a Saturday, Mummy gave us a strong dose of Castor Oil to purge our bodies of toxic substances. It was always a horrible experience for us because we hated the taste of the Castor Oil, and always vehemently resisted taking it.

She always administered the Castor Oil sequentially beginning with the oldest child and ending with me, the youngest. That day, my brother resisted more than he ever did before. He was crying and pushing away the spoon, and spilled the Castor Oil on the floor. He ran through the back door and around the house with my parents chasing him. They grabbed him and brought him back into the house. My father lay my brother down on one of the school benches and sat on him while my mother forced his mouth open and poured the Castor Oil down his throat. He swallowed most of it, but he also spit up some on my mother's shirt.

Daddy took out the leather belt and began to beat him. My father did not beat me as often as my mother, but when he did it was a violent beating. He did not care where the belt landed. He would flay the belt angrily and it would land on any part of my body – face, back, arms, neck.....anywhere. I became terrified, and not knowing what my fate would be when it was my turn to take the Castor Oil, I bolted for the door. Mummy grabbed the broom and ran behind me. As I was running around the house, she beat me in my head with the broom handle. She overpowered me, took me back inside and forced the Castor Oil down my throat.

At other times, Mummy punished me by making me kneel down in the back yard on the concrete floor in the scorching sun for long periods. Mummy was always angry with me. I never knew what would make her mad at me, so I tried to do and say everything right. But no matter what I did or said, she found fault with me.

All my life I tried to please her, but I never could. I felt so hurt and rejected and could not understand why my mother hated me so much. I wondered what I did to make her hate me. Often I felt that I was adopted. It just wasn't possible, I surmised, that I could really be her daughter. Had it not been for the fact that I looked exactly like her, I would have believed this. It was only when I was sixteen that I discovered exactly why she hated me.

Chapter 5
Running Away From Home

My siblings and I attended my grandmother's kindergarten, which was ideally located in our house. We then went on to attend Tranquility Government Primary School. My sister, being the eldest, graduated before I started primary school.

By the time I entered primary school at age six, I was shy and afraid of people. But at home, when I played with my friends in the kindergarten and in the neighborhood, I was different. By the time I reached my 2nd year, I had adapted to primary school and played happily and noisily in the school yard with the other kids.

In my fourth year of primary school, my new teacher was Mrs. Thomas. Mrs. Thomas was a friend of my mother's, and lived on a street near to our house. On the first day of class, Mrs. Thomas called me out and sternly rebuked me in front the entire class. She said that my mother told her that I was a bad child and that I gave a lot of trouble at home. My mother, she said, also told her that I was "no good" and would "never amount to anything". Mrs. Thomas said that she had been waiting three years for me to be in her class so she could punish me, and that my mother was the one who told her to do so. She droned on and on about how horrible I was, while my classmates began to laugh at me and look at me with scorn. I was hurt, confused and humiliated. What do I do, I wondered, that was so horrible that my mother would say those things about me?

Mrs. Thomas made good on her threat. She ridiculed me and verbally abused me as often as possible. Since my mother had also given her permission to beat me, she did so at every opportunity. One day she beat me with a wooden ruler because my answer to an arithmetic problem was wrong. The ruler had a razor-sharp embedded metal strip that protruded from its side. Mrs. Thomas beat me with the metal side of the ruler, cutting my hand and causing it to bleed. In spite of the abuse at home and at school, I always had good grades.

When I was eight years old, I tried to run away from home. I was very unhappy and did not want to live with my family anymore. I had nowhere to go, but I packed a tiny bag with a few belongings, including my favorite doll, and walked up the street. I got no further than the home of our family friends, the Josephs. It began to get dark, and realizing that I could not live with the Josephs, I went back home. My mother gave me a severe beating.

The problems in our family grew worse. Grandmummy and Mummy continued to fight, Daddy continued to sleep with other women, and the arguments and contention between them exacerbated. One day Mummy found tangible proof of an affair my father was having with a woman she knew. Mummy confronted the woman, and Daddy became enraged. Subsequently, Daddy packed a bag and moved out, taking me with him. I was about four years old at the time. He told my mother that he was taking me, and not my brother and sister, because he could not live without me. We went to live with his aunt, Aunty Camilla. I could not understand why I could no longer live with the rest of the family. I felt confused and hurt and that I was to blame for the separation. After only a couple weeks, we moved back home.

Chapter 6
Please Don't Kill The Kittens

Grand mummy, my father's mother, was a battle ax. She was sharp tongued, combative and domineering. While I was afraid of both her and my mother, there was something sinister about Grandmummy that scared me. Grandmummy loved cats. The cats were constantly reproducing, so there were always these cute little kittens running through our house. At one time, Grandmummy had fourteen cats. Whenever there were too many kittens, Grandmummy would dispose of them in an unorthodox manner.

One day, she gathered up the kittens, placed them in a cardboard box and took me for a walk. I walked along the street, holding her hand and skipping along, as she carried the box of kittens. Suddenly we came to the river that was obliquely across the street from our house. She placed the box on the river bank, took the kittens out of the box, one at a time, and flung them into the river where they drowned. I was petrified and began crying hysterically, but Grandmummy ignored me, and dragged me back home. Over the next few years, she took me with her each time she went to drown the kittens. When I became older, I wondered why she always took me down to the river with her to kill the kittens.

Grandmummy also hated me. I know now that it was because of all the attention my father lavished on me. As a child, I was innocent to the fact that my father treated me differently than the rest of the family. But my mother and grandmother knew, and they both treated me with contempt.

Grandmummy also spoke curses over me. She, like my mother, said that I would never get married and that no one would ever want me. She complained to my father about me at every opportunity. My life was such that I became afraid to do or say anything because I did not know what would displease Mummy and Grand mummy. I loved my entire family very much, and could not understand why I was treated differently.

When I was a young child, Grandmummy went to England to visit her son Earl, his wife Glenda and their children. In those days international travel was a privileged experience. Grandmummy made a special outfit for the occasion..... a tailored navy blue suit with white gloves, white shoes and white hat. The entire family went to see her off. It was a splendid event, and we all experienced the trip vicariously through Grand mummy.

Grandmummy stayed in England for several months. During her visit, she told her daughter-in-law, Glenda, that I was a prostitute. I was only eleven years old at the time! My Aunt Glenda unwittingly believed my grandmother's lie. Aunt

Glenda began to dislike me and thereafter, any time she came to Trinidad to visit she treated me badly.

When I was thirty-two years old, Aunt Glenda apologized to me for believing my grandmother, and for disliking me because of the lies she told her about me when I was just eleven years old.

I began attending high school at the age of eleven. In Trinidad and Tobago, you have to take an entrance test to get into high school. Students have to indicate their five high school choices ranging from their first selection to their last. Placement hinges on the test score the student obtains. I wanted to attend Holy Name Convent, the same high school my sister attended because I wanted to be like her. After all, hadn't my mother always told me "why can't you be like your sister?" I construed that if I became like my sister then my mother would love me. I was elated to learn that because of my test score, I was placed in my first school of choice, Holy Name Convent.

Although I was excited to attend high school, the environment was very alien to me. The nuns were very strict, and the rules were multitudinous. Strict adherence to the rules was expected, and any deviance from those rules resulted in open chastisement. As expected of any young lady, especially one that was convent educated, we had to conduct ourselves at all times in a highly exemplary manner. It was absolutely forbidden to be in the presence of any males after school while we were in uniform.

Our uniforms consisted of a short sleeved white shirt, blue tie, white shoes, white socks and a gray pleated skirt which had to be several inches below the knee. We had to wear a whole - slip and not a half-slip, because our bras must never be visible through our shirts. Absolutely no jewelry was permitted. Our hair and nails had to be well groomed, and our clothes had to be immaculate.

At random times, the nuns would have a surprise inspection. Armed with their tape measures, they would measure the length of our skirts, check to see whether we were wearing a whole slip, and inspected our hair, nails and overall appearance.

During my first year of high school, I was terribly shy and had only one friend. I was very quiet and seldom talked with anyone. I was an avid student who enjoyed studying and discovering all the new things I was learning. At the end of the first semester, there was an open house where parents were invited to come and discuss the progress of their children. My mother attended, and met with my homeroom teacher,
Sister K.

In my presence, Sister K told Mummy that I was loud, unruly and disobedient! She further said that I was a terrible student who, in her opinion, would never succeed at anything. I listened, aghast, as Sister K continued to lie to my mother.

I could not believe that this nun would speak so many lies about me to Mummy.

Pointlessly, when I told my mother that I did none of the things that Sister K said I did, Mummy believed her and not me. I was severely punished when we went home.

When I was older, I learned that my mother had called Sister K before the open house, and told her to say those untruthful things about me in order to punish me.

Despite this incident, my high school education, for the most part, went reasonably well. On occasion, I was chastised for things like talking too much during class or for not turning in my homework on time.

Education at the convent was very balanced and aimed at producing well adjusted, capable, marriage ready and academically educated women. My core courses, which were required of each student, were elocution (the art of effective public speaking, proper diction, and the proper use of gestures, stance, and dress), art, etiquette, protocol, cooking, sewing, singing, Latin, and Religious Instruction.

Religious Instruction was one of my most interesting subjects. I wanted to learn about God - who He was and why He created us. However, we were not allowed to ask any questions in the class. One day I ventured bravely and asked "why doesn't God answer our prayers?" To which my teacher, Sister H angrily replied "Who says He doesn't? An answer can be yes or no!"

Her answer made me very sad. I wondered why God had not answered "yes" to my prayers. I had asked Him so many times to let my mother love me, but God did not answer my prayer. Surely, I thought, this was a good request that God would want to answer, wouldn't He?

Notwithstanding, I began to sense the presence of God at a very young age although I had not yet become a born again Christian. I would be in a room and sense that He was right there with me. I know now that the Lord's hand was upon me from the time I was conceived.

Life in the Harris household became unhappily predictable. Daddy continued to commit adultery. Grandmummy and Mummy continued to hate each other and vie for daddy's attention. And Grandmummy and Mummy continued to dislike me. My siblings and I did not get along well with each other. Mummy embarrassed Daddy and ridiculed him among relatives, and friends and when they were out in the general public.

Mummy and Daddy argued over his incessant sexual liaisons and his relationship with Grand mummy, and me. At the age of 12, Mummy and Daddy complained to me separately about each other's behavior. Daddy complained to me that Mummy was a horrible person, and he related things that took place in their marriage. Mummy complained to me about Daddy's infidelity and his obsession with my grandmother.

Their goal in discrediting each other was to force me to take sides, thereby choosing one of them over the other. I loved both my parents very much, and did not want to take sides. Instead, I encouraged them to love and forgive each other. They would each get angry with me and accuse me of loving one more than the other. Consequently, I felt that I was to blame for the breakdown of their marriage. The load and responsibility of trying to fix my parents' marriage were too great for me to bear. At the age of twelve, I felt like I was a marriage counselor, and an unsuccessful one at that.

Chapter 7
Memorable Moments

In spite of my traumatic home environment, I still had some memorable events during my childhood. Daddy loved to take the family for a drive in his car in the evenings or on the weekends. He usually drove west to the suburban towns of Diego Martin and Carenage. The Diego Martin valley lies just west of the capital, Port of Spain, where we lived and east of Carenage, a small bustling seaside town. Daddy loved to drive to the newly developing area of Diamond Vale, a housing development that lay in the heart of the Diego Martin valley. His desire was to buy land there and build us a new home. And he did. In 1967, Daddy bought a parcel of land in Diamond Vale and personally designed our new house. We moved into the new house in 1968.

Our parents often took us to the coastal village of Mayaro which is on the east coast of Trinidad. The main attraction in Mayaro is the beach which is a popular destination for long weekends, holidays and vacations. The beach is lined with an array of coconut trees, as proof of the days when most of the area consisted of coconut plantations. We sometimes spent holidays, weekends and summer vacations in Mayaro. We would get up early, around 4:00 am, and leave the house by

5:00 am. The drive took over two hours, so we, the children, would get impatient because we longed to get there. When we finally saw the first set of coconut trees, a sure indication that we were close, my brother would begin to sing a song he composed about Mayaro.

We always stayed at Aunty Dora, my mother's cousin. We played on the beach, and swam and rollicked in the water. All too soon, it seemed, it was always time to leave and go back home.

Another memorable part of my childhood was my visits to my aunt's house. Aunty Elaine, Mummy's sister, lived with her husband, Uncle Eric around the corner from our house. She had 11 children, two girls and nine boys. Their home was warm and welcoming. Theirs was a loving home where friends and families loved to congregate. Aunty Elaine was a kind, sweet, loving woman, and a great mother. I loved spending time with her, and all my cousins. But I was afraid to tell her, or anyone else, what I was enduring at home.

I also enjoyed being with my grandfather, who also lived close by. Granddaddy was a very warm and loving man, and I loved him very much. Each Sunday morning, after church, my siblings and I would visit him. He was always delighted to see us. Granddaddy, who lived alone, would fix us a great homemade breakfast. We would spend time talking with him, reading the comic page of the newspaper and picking cherries from the tree in his back yard.

Granddaddy visited his two daughters, Yvonne and Elaine, every evening. He never visited one without visiting the other because he did not want them to feel alienated. First, he would walk to Aunty Elaine's house which was the closest to him, and would spend a couple hours there. He then walked to our house where he would sit in his favorite chair and watch television.

Granddaddy never talked a lot, but just being in his quiet presence made me feel safe. I loved to climb up in his lap and hug him. He always smelled of peppermint and Old Spice cologne. Granddaddy died when I was eleven, and I was devastated.

My godparents, Aunty Marge, who was my mother's first cousin, and her husband Uncle Vernon, lived a few blocks from our house. Sometimes my parents would allow me to walk to their house to visit them. Aunty Marge was an excellent cake decorator. I loved to sit with her and watch her ice and decorate wedding cakes, birthday cakes and other special occasion cakes. She wanted to teach me how to do it, but I declined. Later, I wished that I had said yes.

Aunty Marge and Uncle Vernon were sweet and loving. They had no children, but their home was filled with their family's children who they had informally adopted. Aunty Marge's home was cozy. She had numerous plants throughout the house, family pictures on the wall, and beautiful flowers adorning various rooms in the house.

I had a wonderful relationship with my godparents. They loved me and I loved them. I wished that I could live with them, and often told Aunty Marge so.

As a young child, I felt closer to my father because I had a better relationship with him than the other members of my family, but as a teenager all that changed. As a teenager, I was becoming a young woman, which to my father meant that boys would begin to be attracted to me. My father became strict and absolutely refused to let me talk to boys. On the other hand, my sister Leslie was allowed to date at the age of fourteen and even had a steady boyfriend at that age. However, I was so shy and afraid of being rejected that the possibility of me having a boyfriend was remote.

Because I was rejected by my mother, I felt that everyone else would reject me. Mummy took every opportunity to reject my love for her. I would often tell her how much I loved her, and would try to hug and kiss her, but she would not reciprocate. She continued to abuse me, ridiculing and embarrassing me at every opportunity.

During high school, I would walk to my mother's job after school where my father picked us up and drove us home. Since school got out at 2:30 pm, I usually got to my mother's job by 3:00 pm. I only had to wait about an hour and a half before Mummy finished work and Daddy picked us up. I passed the time by walking through the department store where Mummy worked, and looked at all the merchandise.

Mummy had a lot of friends at the department store. Once, I was in the store with Mummy as she casually chatted with some of them. One of them said something to me, and I smiled. Mummy looked at me and said, "Your teeth are so yellow". Humiliated and hurt, I walked away crying.

Two of my school mates, Allison and Rhonda lived near our new house in Diamond Vale. Daddy gave them a ride to school in the mornings, along with Mummy, Leslie, Alan and me. Because the car could hold only five passengers, Allison and Rhonda took turns riding with us. The sisters were very shy and quiet, and seldom spoke when they rode in the car with us.

On one particular morning, Mummy was in the mood to humiliate me because I was late getting ready for school. She waited until we were in the car to berate me just so that she could embarrass me in Rhonda's presence. She insulted me all the way to school saying, "You are so nasty". "You do not even bathe". "You don't even brush your teeth". "Your underwear is so dirty". "You don't even wash them". She went on and on with the lies and insults while we all sat in silence as no one dared say a word. I cringed and cried inside. By the time I got to school I was emotionally ruined.

I looked forward to the times when I was sick because it was at those times that my mother would sometimes pay me some semblance of attention. To me, attention was equated with love, so I relished those times when I was sick and she took care of me. However, there were times when she did not.

On one occasion, when I was about ten years old, I told Mummy that I was feeling sick and needed to lie down. She refused, and made me clean the kitchen. I cleaned the kitchen, but had to stop at several intervals as I became ill and had to keep running to the bathroom to vomit. Mummy watched the whole episode, but forced me to continue working.

Chapter 8
Why Daddy Why?

As a teenager, Leslie, Alan and I joined the Diamond Vale Youth Club. The club was a great place to meet and socialize with other young people. My sister and I became friends with several of the club's members, and soon we became part of a popular clique. Our new friends' parents were also friends of our parents. Consequently, Mummy and Daddy allowed us to pursue our friendships with them. We had parties at our home, and attended parties held at our friends' homes. The only reason I was allowed to attend the parties was because my sister accompanied me. I was not allowed to go anywhere unless my sister went with me. Daddy drove us to the parties and picked us up at a time of his choosing.

Daddy was very strict with me, but not with my sister and brother. He had a list of things I could not do. I was not allowed to date, not even when I was in my late twenties. I could not talk to boys. I could not go anywhere by myself until I was 18, and even then that was a problem. I was not allowed to associate with any of my friends who as he put it "did not belong to our class". Not only did I have to endure my father's strict behavior, but I had to deal with my mother's abuse and dislike of me as well.

When I was sixteen, I found out why my mother hated me. Mummy told her friend, Brenda, who lived across the street from us that I had been having an affair with my father since I was a young child! My mother was so convincing that the neighbor hated me and treated me horribly almost all my life.

The truth is that as a child, my father drugged and raped me repeatedly. My mother knew and did nothing about it. Instead, she hated me and believed that I was actually having an affair with my father……..that I was willfully and knowingly having sex with him!

When I was older, and I finally got her to talk about it, she told me that she used to see Daddy go into my bedroom, lock the door, and stay in my room for a long time. My mother never confronted him about it, nor did she try to stop it. Instead, she treated me like I was "the other woman". I became her enemy, and someone with whom she felt she had to compete with all her life. She opposed everything I said or did. She was hostile and angry with me all my life because she actually believed that I was having an affair with my father.

When I was in my thirties, a friend of my father's told me, that Daddy confessed to them that he used to drug me with chloroform and rape me. Chloroform, which is a colorless liquid, is a dangerous drug. It was used before the 1900s as an anesthetic, and to render a victim unconscious. It can cause death from paralysis of the heart, and also depresses most of the body's other organs including the kidneys, liver, blood vessels and pancreas. It is also toxic to the liver. Chloroform was widely used in cough syrups, liniments, sedatives, and pain relievers. Since 1976, it was banned from being used in drug, cosmetic, and food products, and is listed as a carcinogen by the U.S. Environmental Protection Agency. It was a miracle that I was not permanently damaged by my father drugging me with it.

I always loved children. In high school, I wanted to have twelve children of my own as well as have an orphanage where I would care for all the abused and hurting children. I baby-sat almost all the children on our street, and was particularly fond of our next door neighbor's little boy, William. He was a cute, chubby eight month old baby when his parents moved next door to us. I used to bathe him, powder and diaper him and rock him to sleep. I loved him like he was my baby boy.

When he was five years old, he said something startling to me. I was instructing him to do something, and like a typical child, he did not want to do it. It was then he said to me, "Your mother said you will never get married. No one will ever love you". I was stupefied. Mummy had actually spoken ill of me to a five year old boy –and not just any five year old boy, but one with whom I had a delightful relationship. This was another one of her attempts to discredit me with everyone that I cared for.

I looked forward to when I graduated from high school because I thought that as an adult I would be free from the bondage, rejection and abuse I suffered from both my parents. But that did not happen.

I graduated from high school when I was just sixteen, and still too young to make my own decisions. I looked forward to attending the traditional graduation ball where students dressed in beautiful formal gowns and were escorted by their dates. At the start of my senior year, I talked about the ball with my parents, expressing to them what I wanted to wear. As the graduation ball drew near, I waited expectantly to see if they had gotten my gown. About a month before graduation, Daddy told me that I was not going to the ball. He refused to let me go because he did not want me going out with a boy. I cried and cried, but it did not move him. Everyone in my graduating class attended the ball except me.

I had my first nervous breakdown when I was sixteen. A month after I graduated from high school, my classmate Joan invited me to her house for the weekend. Joan was one of my best friends. She lived in a blue-collar neighborhood a few miles from us. I had been to her house before, but had never spent a weekend. Daddy drove me there a couple times and picked me up after the visit. This time, because I was going to spend the weekend, presented a problem.

Daddy did not want me to go because he felt that a weekend would give me too much freedom to meet and mingle with the boys in the neighborhood. I begged and pleaded, and finally he consented.

On my way to Joan's house, Daddy pounded his fist angrily on the steering wheel and screamed loudly at me. "I do not want you to go there", he shouted. "I do not want you to associate with those poor nappy headed black losers in that neighborhood. You are to stay in the house for the entire weekend. Do not even go on the porch. Do not talk to any boys. If you do, I will find out and beat you". When my father got angry, he got into a terrifying rage where he threw things, cursed and screamed loudly. His face contorted with rage, his nostrils flared and his eyes glared maniacally.

As he raged on, I bawled hysterically. I could not handle anymore. Everything that I had been through came to a climax, and I simply felt no longer able to cope. I told him that if those were the criteria, I no longer wanted to go to Joan's house. He turned the car around and took me back home.

We entered the house with me screaming and shaking uncontrollably and Daddy shouting loudly at me. I walked past my mother, who was in the kitchen, into my bedroom with Daddy following me.

A torrent of words exploded from my mouth. It was as though a dam had broken. All my repressed emotions were released and I began to tell him how unhappy and depressed I had been and that I did not want to live at home anymore.

I bolted out of my bedroom, down the corridor and into the kitchen, with the intention of running out of the house and never coming back. But I got no further than the kitchen.

Mummy had a filled a bucket of water and was waiting for me. As I ran past her in the kitchen, she picked up the bucket and threw the water on me like I was a dog. I slipped and fell, soaking wet, in the water, but not before I saw the smirk on her face. She was delighted that Daddy was angry with me. I had a nervous breakdown, the first of what would be many in the years ahead.

Hoping to gain my independence, I began working shortly after my graduation, at age sixteen, at a major government agency. I enjoyed my job and actually looked forward to going to work each day.

Shortly after I began working, I had another nervous breakdown while at work. An attack of depression and anxiety descended upon me so severely that I could not function normally or think clearly. A weakness assailed my body and I went into a bout of uncontrollable crying. My face became deathly pale, and my body trembled violently. I thought I was dying. My boss and co-workers were afraid and did not know what to do. Someone decided to call my father and have him come and take me home.

Daddy was there in less than ten minutes. I lay inconsolably on the back seat of his car as he drove me home. This would become a pattern- me having a nervous breakdown at work and my father being summoned to come and take me home. Sobbing wretchedly, I would ask my family, "Does anybody love me? Someone please tell me you love me."

"Someone please hold me". But they would laugh and dismiss me. Once, the attack was so bad that my parents took me to the doctor who had to sedate me with morphine. I was suffering with depression.

When I was eighteen years old, I had a life-changing experience. My sister, who I had always tried to emulate, came home from work one day and said that she had gotten saved. "Saved?" I asked her. "What does that mean?" She said that she had repented of her sins and had received the Lord Jesus Christ as her personal Savior. She said that I too needed to repent of my sins and receive Jesus Christ as my personal Savior, so that I could spend eternity in heaven. The only way to heaven, she said, was by personal faith in Jesus Christ.

I was a devout Catholic. I attended a convent high school and mass every Sunday. I had taken catechism classes and had my First Communion and Confirmation. I was a "good person". I believed in the Ten Commandments and had never heard about salvation through Jesus Christ. I was intrigued, but did not quite understand what it all meant.

My sister changed overnight. She was happier, her character was changing, and she began attending a born-again Christian Church. She urged me to get saved.

I was not ready to give my life to the Lord because there were so many things I wanted to do that I had not yet been allowed by my parents to do.

I wanted to go to parties, have some fun and have a boyfriend.

At eighteen, my life was very sheltered. I did not know how to take a taxi, as my father did not allow me to. I could not date. I did not know anything about sex. I thought that men had a menstrual cycle! I was so shy and insecure that if anyone looked at me I cried. And I suffered with rejection. I wanted to enjoy life, and then, when I was old or just before I died, I would give my life to the Lord. I also concluded that I was a "good person", and therefore would surely make it into heaven.

I had become friends with one of my co-workers, Cindy and her cousin Wendy. Cindy and Wendy were part of the "in-crowd". They always wore the hottest fashions and knew all the latest dances. We hung out, without my father knowing, with an elite group of guys and girls and attended house parties. My father still drove me to the parties and picked me up. I usually had to leave earlier than anyone else because Daddy always picked me up early. I would hear him honking his horn when he pulled up, and I had to leave immediately or he would come in the house to get me, which would greatly embarrass me. Sometimes, if I begged really hard, he would allow me to leave the party with my friends.

One day, one of the guys from our group came over, unexpectedly, to our house to visit me. He was dark-skinned and had an Afro hairstyle. Daddy came home and saw me sitting in the living room talking with the guy, and told me he wanted to speak with me immediately. I got up from the chair, and went into the kitchen to talk with him.

Daddy was very angry with me and said, "What is that black (he actually used the N word) no-good boy doing in my house? I do not want you hanging around him. He looks like he digs dirt on a construction site. I want him out of my house NOW! Is that your boyfriend?" I assured my father that he was just a friend and NOT my boyfriend, but Daddy did not believe me. I was forced to ask my friend to leave.

Although I was part of this really "cool" group, I did not fit in. I did not act like them or talk like them, and I felt so insecure, worthless and unfilled all the time. I constantly tried to prove my worthiness by saying and doing the right things, but the barrenness I felt inside would not dissipate. I wanted to be happy. I wanted to be loved. Then I met Kevin, who fell in love with me. Kevin had recently returned to Trinidad from living in the United States. We were introduced to each other by one of the guys in our group. We were instantly attracted to each other and began dating secretly, so my father would not find out.

Meanwhile, my sister met and married her husband, and moved out of the house. My brother met his wife-to-be, with whom I became best friends. Although she was only two years older than me, She became like a surrogate mother to me. She taught me how to do a lot of things, including how to take a taxi.

The same year I turned eighteen, Mummy took me to see her doctor because I had the flu. Dr. Ellison was a general practitioner who my mother thought was an excellent doctor. He had been her doctor for many years, and she was very comfortable with him. The only problem being his patient was that you had to wait very long in the waiting room before your name was called because he took an unusually long time with most of his patients.

On this particular day, Mummy went in to Dr. Ellison's office with me. After discussing my condition with him, he asked my mother to leave so he could examine me. Although he was not a gynecologist or an obstetrician, Dr. Ellison proceeded to give me a gynecological exam. It was my first time having one, so I did not know what to expect.

A few minutes into the exam, I noticed that Dr. Ellison's demeanor had changed. He was breathing heavily. When I realized that something was wrong, I immediately told him to stop. In short, Dr. Ellison molested me in his office. I never told my mother what happened in that office because I was afraid of what she would do. Years later, Dr. Ellison was arrested for raping a female patient. He left the country to avoid prosecution.

In the summer of 1974, and almost three weeks after Kevin and I began dating, my sister invited me to a special service at her Church. I accepted the invitation. The service was unlike any other church service I had ever attended. The people were friendly and welcoming. After the worship, the visiting speaker got up to speak. Every single argument that I had given for not being ready to receive Jesus Christ as my Lord and Savior was presented almost verbatim by the speaker. At some point I thought that my sister had given the speaker all that information about me. But then I realized that I had not even shared any information with her as to why I was not ready to be saved.

The speaker began to explain the gospel of the Kingdom of God-which is that all mankind is born in sin, our sin separates us from God, and Jesus Christ died to redeem us from our sins. He described the wounding and brutally painful death that Jesus suffered to set us free. By repenting of our sins and receiving Jesus Christ into our lives as our Lord and Savior, he further said, we become saved or born-again.

I sat in the pew and listened intently to the account of Jesus' suffering on the Cross for my sins, and that there was nothing good in me that would reconcile me to God. I wept silently. My heart broke. I whispered internally "Oh Jesus. I did not know. I did not know that you died for me. I did not know how much you suffered because you love me. I am so sorry Lord. Please forgive me". As I said those words, I immediately saw a mist hovering over me. Ever so gently, it came closer and closer to me and engulfed me. It was the Holy Spirit.

My sister's Church did not believe in altar calls – that is inviting people to come up to the altar and make a public confession of their faith. That being the case, the service came to a close by the speaker saying that anyone who wanted to be saved should talk to any member of the congregation after the service. When the service concluded, everyone became engrossed in chatting with each other, so I left without being able to tell anyone there what had happened.

At home, the first person I told was my sister. She was elated. The next day, I met with Kevin and told him that I was breaking off the relationship because I was now a born-again Christian. No one told me to do this. I just knew that there was no way I could be a Christian and still date him. He was, understandably, very angry.

At work, people began noticing the change in me. I began to tell everyone about my experience and encouraged them to also give their lives to the Lord. And I joined my sister's Church.

For the first six months after I was saved, everything was euphoric. I told everyone I knew about the Lord. The change in me was evident to all who knew me. I was joyful and at peace for the first time in my life.

But, after six months, the depression re-surfaced. I was miserable and was being troubled with suicidal thoughts. Although I had changed, nothing in my life had. There were still the same problems at home.

Everyone in the Church seemed so perfect, so I was embarrassed to tell anyone how I was feeling, lest they condemned me. But one day, when I felt I could not cope, I told an older woman who was a leader in the Church, "I feel so depressed", to which she replied "But, you shouldn't be". I repeated it and she repeated "But, you shouldn't be". We continued back and forth like this without her ever helping me. I concluded that if I shouldn't be depressed, and I AM depressed, maybe there was something wrong with me.

Chapter 9
Looking For Love
.......In All The Wrong Places

Grandmummy died two years after I got saved. She was ill for quite some time with stomach cancer. She deteriorated to a place where she was unable to bathe or clothe herself. She lay in her bed all day long in pain. Daddy asked my mother to bathe her and put on her clothes, but Mummy refused. The task fell to me.

I used to bathe her, comb her hair, and dress and feed her. Before she became ill, I used to share the gospel with her, hoping that she would give her life to the Lord. But she always belligerently refused. When she became critically ill, I approached her again about becoming saved. This time she listened. She repented of her sins and asked Jesus Christ to come into her heart. She died two weeks later. Just before she died, she asked my mother to forgive her for all that she did to her.

During the next few years, I continued to attend Church regularly, joined the choir, and became a Sunday School teacher and a Christian camp counselor. I formed a children's ministry, and taught Bible school at our home on Saturdays to all the children who lived on our street. I also led my sister-in-law to the Lord and then my mother. My brother soon followed, but not my father. I read my Bible and prayed, but was still depressed.

I had the head knowledge that God loved me, but I did not feel it in my heart. I longed to experience the Lord in an intimate way, but was unable to. I could not see God as Father because I transferred my knowledge of fatherhood, arising from the abusive relationship between my father and me, unto the Lord. In addition, the rejection from my mother transferred into all my relationships with people, casual or intimate.

Although my mother had become saved, she still continued to treat me despicably. Mummy regularly threatened to place me in a home for juvenile delinquent girls. I lived with this fear for several years. I was afraid to do or say anything for fear of my mother's and others' rejection, lack of acceptance, or disapproval.

Rejection is an emotionally, mentally and physically debilitating experience that causes a person to feel worthless and unloved, and thus often results in self-rejection. Rejection is the refusal to accept, recognize or give affection to a person. There are even more devastating results when the rejection is done by a parent. With rejection also comes the fear of rejection which is the belief that people will not accept you for who you are. The rejected person's behavior then becomes very cautious, always wanting to please people by doing or saying what they want with the goal of being accepted and loved.

Years later I would learn that I was also being oppressed with spirits of rejection, self-rejection, fear of rejection, abuse, incest and other demonic strongholds.

Satan, the arch-enemy of God and his demonic horde of fallen angels oppress people, saved and unsaved. The enemy preys upon both the strong and the weak. Demonic spirits oppress people regardless of their innocence and vulnerability. These spirits strategically and maliciously oppress or possess people, tormenting them and creating havoc in their lives. Spirits of rejection, spirits of fear of rejection and spirits of abuse also influence people to reject and abuse the oppressed person. There are numerous accounts in the Bible where Jesus cast out demonic spirits from people. However, the Church we were attending did not believe in deliverance.

As the pain of rejection and abuse continued to exacerbate, I grew more and more discontented and depressed. I expected so much more to happen in my life by becoming a Christian. My local Church, where I had gotten saved, was legalistic, archaic and steeped in man-made doctrines and traditions. The women were not allowed to speak during church services, not even to ask a question during bible study. Absolutely no makeup or jewelry was allowed, except for a wedding ring, and the women's hair had to be kept covered during the service.

The worship service consisted of ancient hymns that were sung at a deadly slow pace. Musical instruments were not allowed, except for a piano which was only played on Sundays. They did not teach on the intimacy of the Lord, nor were there any manifestations of the glorious presence of God in any of the services. They believed that healing and deliverance was not for the present-day Church. And they did not believe in the baptism of the Holy Spirit with the evidence of speaking in tongues.

I not only wanted to experience more of the Lord, but I needed to be delivered from my afflictions. I could not get any help from my local Church so I visited other Churches and tried to get help from them. But those whom I told that there was something wrong with me, disagreed and said I was okay. But I wasn't.

So, in 1980, dejected and disgusted, I backslid at the age of 24 and left the Church. My sister-in-law, Sonia, and my brother had also become disenchanted with our local Church, so they left too.

Every Friday evening after work and on Saturdays mornings, Sonia and I partied at a local disco in Port-of-Spain. This particular club was the place where the popular young adults hung out. I made up excuses to my parents as to my whereabouts because there would be trouble if they knew what I was doing.

On Fridays, we usually arrived at the club around 5:00pm and left around 9:00pm. On Saturdays, we got there around 9:00am and stayed for about three hours. I did not drink or smoke, but I loved to dance. To others I must have looked like I was having a great time, but I was miserable. I was always looking around carefully as we entered the club because I did not want anyone who knew I was a Christian see me. I felt so guilty and uncomfortable about what I was doing. But I was not ready to stop. I wanted to fill the void inside me with partying, dancing and hanging out with the popular crowd. But the rejection I felt was still there, masked temporarily when I was out having fun.

When you are suffering with rejection, you are constantly craving to be loved. Oftentimes, rejected people substitute sex for love. To them, sex is a form of love. But sex is a poor, deceptive substitute for love because it never satisfies. I remember once that a friend told me that men would only want me because of my body, and would never really love me. I wanted to be loved, and if I couldn't be loved, having sex would work just as well..... or so I thought.

So I began having sex, but felt nothing physically or emotionally. But still I continued. As the song by Marc Almond says, I kept "looking for love in all the wrong places". The lyrics of that song aptly sum up the futility of what I was doing.

Looking For Love In All The Wrong Places
By Marc Almond
(Source: http://www.metrolyrics.com)

Keep on looking now

You gotta keep on looking now

Keep on looking now

You're looking for love

In all the wrong places

Where your walk it's always shadow

Conversation always shallow

When they talk they never look you in the eye

They look over your shoulder

To faces even colder

And you feel a little older

Every time

You're looking for love

In all the wrong places

When you're looking for reaction

When you're searching for direction

When you're scared of rejection

Or attack
You need the warmth of loving
When you're growing tired of seeing
A colourless reflection
Looking back

You're looking for love
In all the wrong places

Something real to fill those little empty spaces
So you're looking for love in all the wrong places

You need understanding
You need a home
All those people so alone
You need understanding
You need a home
All those people so alone

You're looking for love
In all the wrong places
You're looking for love
In all the wrong places
You better keep on looking now!
And so the evening shade will fall
Where nameless voices call and call

And think of all the friends you made
While you toast with Prozac and lemonade

You can hold me under septic skies
(You can dream to your own places)
Watch the sun set in my eyes
(You can't seem to put)
Could this be the time to die?
(A name to all the faces)
The wind upon your face
(Something real)
Your lips upon my lips
Like urban velvet
(To fill those little empty spaces)

So you're looking for love in all the wrong places
You keep on looking for love in all the wrong places

Dream and take away the tears
(Keep on looking now)
Drift on to where your heart is numb
(You gotta keep on looking now)
It's lovely there where love becomes
A drug to fill your need
Just believe in you!

And learn to love yourself
Before anyone else

Chapter 10
Stalked........and Beaten

For some reason men, young and old, black and white, rich and poor, were attracted to me. Older men, including my parents' friends who lived on our street, made advances towards me, and it disgusted and terrified me. I was afraid of older men because they reminded me of my father and what he did to me. Consequently, all the boyfriends I ever had were always younger than me.

All I ever wanted was to have a real home and family with a husband and children. I searched for this almost all my life. I viewed each man with whom I had a relationship to be a potential husband. I thought that each one of them would marry me and that we would "live happily ever after". Some of the relationships lasted as little as three weeks …….and not by my own choosing. I experienced a lot of rejection and abuse from these men as well.

Because I was a victim of abuse and rejection, I entered into relationships with men who treated me badly. Like so many women who have been abused and rejected, I did not feel that I deserved to have a relationship with a good man because according to my mother I was a bad person. So I turned down offers from good men and accepted offers from abusive men.

Although I was now twenty-four years old, my father still did not allow me to date. I was still living at home, was working at the same job I had gotten after graduating from high school, and I was contributing financially to the running of the household. I was performing really well on the job, having been promoted to supervisor after being employed for only three months.

I was doing great financially, and bought myself a car. Unknown to me at the time, the moment I bought the car, my father began stalking me. He followed me everywhere I went. If, for example, I told him I was going to my friend, Anne's house, he would drive by her house to see if in fact my car was parked outside her house. Sometimes he would park further up the street and sit in his car for long periods, and follow me when I left one location to see where I went next.

One afternoon, I left the house around 4:00 pm for a date with my boyfriend. I told Daddy that I was going out, but did not tell him where I was going because he would not permit it. Daddy followed me and discovered where I was.

Oblivious to the fact that Daddy knew where I went, I returned home around 11: 00 pm. As I opened the front door, Daddy was waiting for me in the living room. He was enraged. He was yelling and screaming loudly. He accused me of "going out with a boy" and told me that I was a slut.

Suddenly he pounced on me and began to beat me savagely. He punched me repeatedly in my eyes, my face and my stomach. He kicked and punched me in my genital area, and knocked me to the floor repeatedly. By that time I had had enough. I began to fight back, but I could not match his strength and dexterity. I picked up a chair to slam it across his back, but he snatched it from me.

The beating went on for several minutes. The noise could be heard all the way down our street. The only other person at home was my brother. The screaming and commotion woke him. He came running down the hallway yelling to my father, "Leave my sister alone". Simultaneously, I ran into the kitchen and picked up a sharp knife to defend myself. My intention was to stab my father, thereby stopping him from beating me.

My brother ran into the kitchen and wrenched the knife out of my hand. I was sobbing hysterically. He put his arm around me and walked me up and down the street to calm me.

It was so wonderful to have my brother hold and comfort me because that was not something he did. I was the only one in the family that always tried to hug my mother and siblings. My sister did not want me to hug her because she said people would think we were gay. Whenever I tried to hug Alan, he would push me away and say that he felt uncomfortable. It was only when I was older that I understood that they could only equate affectionate gestures with sex because we never experienced any displays of love from our parents.

The beating I endured that night was a turning point in my life. My left eye was permanently weakened, my lip was split and my body ached horribly. I made a decision to leave home, and did so a few weeks after. I moved into a tiny furnished apartment closer to Port-of-Spain. But that proved to be a catastrophe.

My next door neighbor was heavily into witchcraft. Because the walls between our apartments were so thin, I could hear all the rituals and incantations he intoned at night. It was a nightly ritual which began around 10:00pm and continued into the early morning hours. Loud eerie howling and thumping noises resonated from his apartment to mine. And worse than that, an evil presence from his apartment transferred into mine. The atmosphere in my apartment became thick with a pervasive presence of demonic spirits.

A deathly, chilling fear washed over me each night, forcing me to have sleepless nights. I would fall asleep for a few minutes, only to be awakened by the ominous feeling of someone pinning me to the bed. I endured this for three weeks, and reluctantly had to ask my father if he would let me move back home. He delightfully agreed because that would renew the control he had over me.

Things became progressively worse when I moved back home. Daddy continued to manipulate and abuse me mentally and emotionally. One day he came to my job and verbally abused me in front of my staff. I was humiliated and embarrassed. He was very strict and unyielding. When he got angry, he became erratic and out of control. I was terrified of him and my mother.

I did everything I knew to please mummy because I wanted her to love me. But everything I said or did, met with chastisement and ridicule. Sometimes I would take her with me on vacation. I bought her plane ticket, paid for the accommodations and even gave her spending money, but she still complained. I always told her I loved her, but she never reciprocated. Instead she would look at me angrily.

Mummy gave gifts to my siblings and not to me. Once I asked Mummy if I could have her accordion-pleated skirt she used to wear when she was younger. She told me no. A week later she gave it to my sister. Leslie did not like the skirt and gave it to me. When Mummy saw me with the skirt she asked me what I was doing with it. When I told her that Leslie gave it to me, she demanded I take it off. She put it back in her closet. It did not fit her, so it continued to sit in her closet for many years until she eventually threw it away.

My brother and his wife, Sonia, lived at home with us for several years after they married. She and I did a lot of things together. Mummy socialized with us and our friends all the time, even though she was more than twice our ages. She monopolized our conversations and had to be the center of attention when our friends visited. She wanted to go with us everywhere we went, and got angry when she couldn't.

Whenever Sonia and I planned to go out we had to hide it from her. We took our showers and got dressed secretly and then dashed out of the house. When she realized that we were going out she would ask angrily, "Where are you going? "And she would be furious because she could not go with us.

When Mummy was upset with me (and I seldom knew what would make her upset), she often stopped speaking to me for several days. On those occasions, I always tried to converse with her, but she never responded. She kept a stony face and an angry silence. She would not even acknowledge my presence or make eye contact with me. That to me was worse than her speaking to me nastily. I hated the silent treatment because it not only hurt me emotionally and physically, but it made me feel guilty and worthless.

The Silent Treatment is a form of ostracism. When someone is ostracized it affects the part of their brain called the anterior cingulate cortex. The anterior cingulate cortex is the part of the brain that detects pain. When you give someone the silent treatment, you are actually causing that person to feel physical pain! You can actually inflict pain on a person merely by ignoring their existence. The Silent Treatment is torturous and a form of emotional abuse. It is a form of punishment used by abusers. It is also a silent form of anger that expresses to the victim that they do not exist. Abusers often withhold conversation and do not acknowledge another person's existence in order to manipulate them. Victims of the silent treatment often try anything in their power to get back into good grace with the abuser. They often experience a sense of loss, of not belonging, of low self-esteem and a feeling of unworthiness. The silent treatment Mummy subjected me to usually ended when I bought her something nice or did something exceptionally nice for her.

Daddy often told me, "You know your mother hates you". On occasion my friends who visited me at home asked me, "Why does your family treat you so badly?" I never answered their questions, nor did I tell anyone what I was going through. I kept it all the pain locked inside me.

I did not think that anyone would believe me anyway because when my mother was around other people she was cheerful, loving and kind. Mummy giggled a lot and made silly jokes that had everyone laughing. She treated her nieces, nephews and the neighborhood children lovingly.

Those of us who really knew her knew that it was a façade. At home, she was always depressed and sullen. She became restless periodically, and would leave us to go visit friends and family in the United States, Canada and England.

The only person I had confided in about the sexual abuse was my sister-in-law, Sonia. She observed firsthand the way both my parents treated me. There were two other occasions when, desperate for help, I shared my experience. The first occasion was with an older Christian woman with whom I felt safe. She seemed very sympathetic when I shared my story with her. But afterwards, she told several people that if a mother could say that her daughter was having an affair with her father, then it must be true. She labeled me as a liar and a slut.

On the other occasion, I shared openly at a prayer meeting at someone's home that I was in a lot of pain due to an abusive home environment. One of the women at the prayer meeting was a close friend of my father's. She told my father what I said and he was very angry with me. I vowed that I would never tell anyone else.

Chapter 11
Please Let Me Die

By the end of 1980, a new employee came to work in my department. Darren was gentle and kind, and liked me a lot, but I liked him only as a friend. One day, I gave him a ride home after work and he invited me in to meet his family. There was a young Dutchman named Anthony, a close friend of Darren's, who was staying at their home for a few weeks. I became attracted to him, and thought that he liked me as well. But he didn't, and I found that out in the most painful way.

I never had a lasting relationship with a man. In the early stages of the relationship, men loved me ardently, but afterwards they hated me and broke up with me. When I asked them why, each one of them said they did not know, but felt driven to end the relationship. They were as perplexed as I was that they were breaking up with me.

I was rejected by almost every boyfriend I had. They loved me passionately one minute and the next they hated me. Some of them would simply slink away, not telling me that the relationship was over. But others would tell me. Their break-up speech usually began with "I have something to tell you". Then they would tell me that the relationship was over. Over the years I grew deathly afraid whenever a man prefaced a sentence with those six words – "I have something to tell you". I came to understand later that it was because both my mother and grandmother had spoken word curses over me which was that no one would ever want me, and I would never get married.

    The day after I met Anthony, Darren mentioned to me that Anthony said he liked me. Later that week, I went to a party with them. On the way to the party, he began flirting with me in the car. But as soon as we got to the party, he suddenly became interested in another girl there. I was devastated. I was being rejected yet again.

    With a fake smile, I endured the rest of the night in pain, not wanting anyone to know how much I was hurting. I had to take Darren and Anthony home because they rode with me in my car to the party. To my utter consternation, Anthony asked me if I would also give the girl he picked up at the party a ride home. I said yes. During what felt like the longest ride back home, I had to suffer through Anthony and the girl being amorous with each other.

    With everyone dropped off, I went home. As soon as I got there, I rushed into my bedroom and began to weep. I felt that I could not handle any more pain and rejection. I wondered...... what was the point of me living? I wanted my life to end. That night I decided to end it. I wrote a note saying that I was ending my life and why. I then grabbed a bottle of sleeping pills that the doctor had given me to deal with the depression, and swallowed a handful of them. I jumped into the bed, pulled the covers over me and fell asleep.

Around 5:00 pm the next day, my brother realized that I was still sleeping and found it strange. He and my parents burst into my room, saw the sleeping pills and me asleep and panicked. They pulled me off the bed and tried to revive me. Miraculously, I survived. I was still alive!

After that suicide attempt, I decided to renew my relationship with the Lord. I started going back to Church, but this time I went to another local Church within the same denominational organization. My mother, and my siblings and their spouses also moved to the same Church I did.

Although this Church was part of the same organization, it was a little different than the previous Church we attended. There was a wonderful group of young people there with whom we developed a great camaraderie. We had youth meetings and open air outreach services. I was part of a ministry team that did street and door-to door evangelism.

I began teaching Sunday School again at my new Church. I found other outlets, other than my Church, to meet and fellowship with other Christians. I joined Inter-Varsity Christian Fellowship (IVCF) and became a youth counselor and advisor. I was assigned to a local high school where I counseled, trained and equipped young leaders as well as conducted bible studies. I also helped produce the IVCF

Newsletter, and became an integral part of the organization as a camp counselor.

I loved counseling and ministering to young people. Many of them came from abusive homes, and I was able to help them with their problems.

Having these outlets was very therapeutic. It brought about a sense of purpose and fulfillment. However, my local Church still had the same traditions and mindsets. We were indoctrinated to believe that signs, wonders and miracles only happened in biblical times, and were not for the present-day Church. Engaging Satan in spiritual warfare was taboo. The first time I heard a camper at one of the IVCF camps rebuke the enemy, I was shocked and wondered how she could even speak to Satan!

Each Church in the denomination had two or three elders as they did not believe in having pastors. There was no specific elder that was the Church leader. One of the elders, Br. Jones, told me one day that he was in love with me. Br. Jones had a wife and five children, all of whom were members of the Church. I was terrified and angry, and felt foul. I confided in Sonia what he said. Although I verbally and non-verbally spurned him, Br. Jones continued to pursue me for many months. He was an excellent preacher, but he could no longer preach because of his obsession with me. I threatened him that if he did not stop harassing me I would report him to the eldership. He did not stop, so I reported him. I never found out what the outcome was.

At the Church services, only born–again Christians were allowed to sit up front. Non-Christians had to sit at the back of the Church. On Sunday mornings no one was assigned to preach. During the first half of the service there was the usual slow, dragging singing of hymns. No musical instruments were allowed at the morning service, but at the evening service the organ could be played and even guitars. At the evening service, livelier worship songs were allowed.

After the worship at the Sunday morning services, the men prayed spontaneously. After each prayer there was a long silence, and then another man would pray. The prayers were lofty and impersonal. After the prayer session, one or two men stood and shared from the Word of God. This was followed by communion where strong, intoxicating wine was used. Everyone drank from the same cup.

I loved when the youth group at Church got to attend youth conferences in other parts of the country. We would hire a bus to take us. On one occasion, the bus was filled with young people from different Churches within the denomination. For the entire trip, we worshipped the Lord. We sang, clapped, played guitars and drummed on the back of our seats. The atmosphere was filled with the presence of the Lord. There was so much freedom in the Spirit. Everyone was joyful and happy. It was absolutely wonderful. However, word got back to the elders that we had behaved "unruly" on the bus, and had actually drummed on our seats and clapped our hands (drumming and clapping was forbidden). We were chastised and ordered never to do that again.

It was at one of those youth conferences that I met Barbara and Glenda Joseph and their brother Jeffrey. Barbara and I became friends immediately. And I fell in love with Jeffrey. It was a genuine love that took me many years to overcome.

Jeffrey had a striking appearance. People paid attention to him when he walked into a room. He was very charismatic, personable and eloquent. He was a full time minister with a powerful anointing to minister to young people. He led many young people in the country to the Lord. They followed him around like the pied piper. He was a powerful preacher and teacher. Many Christian women, young and old, liked him, and wanted to marry him.

I became very close with Barbara and the rest of the Joseph family, and spent a lot of time at their house. Young people loved to be around the Josephs, so their house was always filled with a lot of people.

Soon I became part of a vibrant group of young Christians. We ministered together at schools and Christian camps. We held neighborhood youth outreaches and rallies. One day we planned to have a youth rally in the eastern part of the country where we would first show an evangelistic film, and then Jeffrey would preach. I told Daddy that I would be going to the rally that Friday night and would be home very late. I assured him that I would be getting a ride back home and would be safe.

The youth rally went later than we expected, as many young people gave their hearts to the Lord. Consequently, I got back home later than I planned. While I was at the youth rally, Daddy had been angrily pacing the floor for hours, knocking on my brother and his wife's bedroom door many times to interrogate them about my whereabouts. Sonia said he behaved like a madman.

When I got home, Daddy was waiting up for me, and almost beat me again. He ranted and raved, and told me that I should have been home earlier. I told him that the meeting went late, but he did not want to hear me. He told me that I was stupid and ignorant. "Who were you out with?" he asked. I told him again that I was at a youth rally, but he refused to believe me. He was screaming so loudly that he woke up everyone in the house. The next morning, he was even angrier than the night before.

When he was angry with me, he had a menacing look in his eyes that terrified me. I was terrified of both he and my mother. I often felt threatened with violence when I was around them. I would shake violently and my heart raced.

I continued to visit the Josephs regularly and enjoyed the times I spent at their house. Everyone expected Jeffrey and I to get married and work in ministry together. Jeffrey and I got along well together, and I genuinely loved him. His family loved me and believed that it was God's will for us to be married.

Barbara and I decided to go to the sister island of Tobago on vacation. While we were there she asked me a very strange question.

She wanted to know if I still believed that it was God's will for Jeffrey and me to be married. I said yes. A few weeks later I found out why she asked me those questions.

One Sunday morning after Church, my friend Odessa asked me the same question. I asked her why she asked me that, to which she replied that Jeffrey was getting married to another woman. My face turned grey. In a trance, I jumped into my car and drove home. I walked into the house and into my bedroom and collapsed on the floor. I screamed and screamed hysterically, writhing in pain on the floor. I hurt so badly that my body actually ached physically. The neighbors peered out of their windows wondering want was happening at our house.

I stopped visiting the Joseph's house, because I could not handle seeing Jeffrey. No one understood what I was feeling. The pain was too great. I shut myself away from anyone who knew the Josephs because I could not bear the pitying stares and comments.

My level of self-esteem had once more dropped to zero. I felt ugly, worthless and ashamed. My face had a perpetual look of pain on it. My eyes were sunken and lifeless. I hated myself and wondered why I was born.

I left IVCF, and stopped being part of the ministry group in which I ministered with Jeffrey. I stopped attending any functions where the Josephs or any other people in the group might be. And I began attending another Church. I received numerous invitations to attend different events, but I declined every one of them. I could not handle the pain of seeing Jeffrey, his family or anyone who was in our circle of friends.

My life became a bleak cycle. I went to work because I had to, and talked only if I had to. After work, I went home, ate, showered and went straight to bed. I lay in bed for hours crying and often unable to sleep. Sometimes I could not sleep at all and on other occasions I slept for hours and hours. I got up the next day and did the same thing all over again. On Sundays I attended Church, but not as regularly as I used to.

It was around that time that I developed Bulimia. I binged on chocolate, cake, cans of frosting, fried chicken and other toxic foods. Then I would take several laxative pills in order to purge my body of the food. This cycle went on for many years.

A couple months after the painful episode with Jeffrey, I received a wedding invitation in the mail. It was an invitation to a double wedding which was to take place between Jeffrey and his fiancée, and Jeffrey's younger sister and her fiancé. How did they expect me to attend? Didn't anyone know that I was unable to cope? Did they really think that I could attend

Jeffrey's wedding, and smile and laugh like nothing had happened? I declined the invitation.

The situation led me to make a crucial decision. I could not risk the pain of running into Jeffrey. I had to leave the country. I decided to pursue a degree in Psychology at the City University of New York (CUNY). I chose psychology because I wanted to understand what was wrong with me and my family. I thought that if I could understand that, I would not only be healed, but I would be able to help my family as well.

I started saving money for university, because as a foreign student I was not entitled to financial aid, and legally would not be able to work. It took about one year, but I finally had enough money for the first year of university. I sold my car and resigned from my job. Daddy was very angry that I was leaving.

As it came nearer to the day for me to leave, Daddy became very hostile towards me. He called me some very nasty names, and told me that I was a fool to leave my job. He told me that I would fail, and would never succeed. The truth was he did not want me to go because he would lose the control he had over me.

The weeks leading up to my departure were very stressful because Daddy's uncontrollable anger towards me was very terrifying. I really needed someone to support me and comfort me. I was a very naïve twenty six year old who was moving to another country to live for four years. I would be supporting myself for the first year of university, and had no money for the subsequent years. But I trusted God to take care of me.

Soon the day came for me to leave. I asked Daddy to give me a ride to the airport, and he angrily said yes. Mummy came as well. The atmosphere in the car was taut. When we arrived at the airport, my father got out of the car, took my three heavy suitcases, threw them on the sidewalk, and got back into the car. I asked him if he would help me with my bags and come into the airport to see me off. He replied angrily "No", and then cursed me.

I struggled into the airport with the bags, and checked in at the ticket counter. I had about a two hour wait until my flight departed, so I sat down in the lounge area. I felt alone, rejected, scared and hurt. The pain was excruciating. Suddenly I looked up and saw my friend Marlene Paulson, walking towards me. Marlene Paulson was one of my co-workers and she was also a Christian. The Lord led her to come to the airport to see me off! She asked me where my family was. "Didn't they come to see you off?" she asked. I told her no. She began to cry, and soon we were both crying. She prayed with me, comforted me and waited until it was time for me to board the plane.

Chapter 12
Moving To America

Although I had visited New York in 1977, I was unprepared for the strangeness I felt in this big city. I was, however, determined to achieve my goal and not let anything or anyone deter me. I kept my focus on the goal, which was to complete my education, and return home to Trinidad.

I enjoyed all my classes, especially Psychology and Communications. Because I always loved the field of Communications, I decided to add Mass Communications as my second major.

However, I was still in a lot of pain over the loss of Jeffrey to another woman. For the first two years of college, I grieved over him. Sometimes the pain of the loss, coupled with the pain of rejection and abuse from my parents, was so heavy that I felt it physically. My head hurt and my body ached. Sometimes I would writhe on the floor crying, in deep pain, unable to find solace. I cried out to God to heal me. I longed to experience God in an intimate way, but I felt there was a block in my life that prevented me from doing so. Something was wrong with me, and I was determined to find out what it was and to be set free from it.

Despite the pain and oppression, I did really well at university. I maintained a straight 'A' average, and was on the Dean's list. For the first three weeks of the first semester I lived with Sonia's sister in Brooklyn. Staying there was not very convenient for me. So when I had the opportunity to move into an apartment with two other women, I took it.

One of these women, Celeste was a very good friend of my sister's, and used to be her neighbor in Trinidad. Celeste and I got along great when she lived in Trinidad. Celeste subsequently migrated to the USA and was sharing an apartment in Brooklyn with two other women, but one them had recently moved out. As they now needed another roommate, Celeste asked me if I would like to share the apartment with herself and Jessica, the remaining roommate. I said yes.

The week after I moved in, I received a distressing letter from my sister warning me not to move in with them because of some distressing news she had heard about Celeste. Celeste had had several hostile altercations with her former roommate.

Although the letter was written several weeks prior to my move, I did not actually receive it until after I moved. I became afraid and really concerned, but because I had nowhere else to go I was forced to stay until I found somewhere else to live.

Celeste, Jessica and I lived in an apartment which had one huge bedroom where we all slept in separate beds. Celeste's four year old daughter, Simone, also lived with us. A few weeks after I moved in, Celeste and Jessica began dropping overtly sexual innuendos intended for me. It was so uncomfortable, that I started dressing in the bathroom daily.

One day when I was taking a shower, Celeste sent her four year old daughter into the bathroom to peek at me. She pulled back the shower curtain, and peered at me. I told her to leave and she ran back into the bedroom. I could hear Celeste asking her, "Did you see her? What did she look like naked?" From that moment I started looking in earnest for a new place to live.

I had made a few friends during my first semester at university. One of them, Carissa, was from my native home of Trinidad. I shared my predicament with her, and she invited me to stay with her temporarily until I found a permanent place to stay. I went home that evening so elated that my situation was resolved. However, that night, things worsened.

Celeste came in from school, looked at the telephone bill and shrieked. She accused me of running up the phone bill, and said that it had never been that high before I had moved in. I did not think that I had run up the phone bill, and could not therefore comprehend why I was being accused of doing so. Even if I was responsible for the high phone bill, I would pay what I owed. My colleagues at school usually called me, and I infrequently called them. I recalled one day when I received a phone call that Celeste commented that it made her really angry that I got more phone calls than she and Jessica. "Why are you more popular than Jessica and I?" she asked angrily. "How come people scarcely call me?" she asked.

That night, Celeste cursed and screamed at me and hurled the pots and pans against the kitchen walls. She behaved so badly that Jessica and I cowered in the bedroom terrified. Jessica eventually went upstairs to visit a neighbor because she could not handle the commotion. I finally ventured into the kitchen to talk to Celeste. She did not want to talk. Instead she threatened to beat me up. I was lucky, she said, that her daughter was there or else she would beat me. Was abuse and rejection destined to persecute me all my life, I wondered? The next morning after Celeste and Jessica left for school, I looked at the phone bill. The bill was eight dollars! I packed my bags and left that night.

I stayed about three weeks at Carissa's apartment, and then moved into my own apartment. I could only afford to pay two months' rent. The money I had saved for university was depleting rapidly, so I asked the Lord to provide me with a job. I had learned that it was legal for a foreign student to work on campus, but not off campus. Miraculously, I got a job as a Peer Counselor in the Student Services department at the university. I enjoyed the opportunities I got to help other students.

One day one of my college friends, a native Trinidadian, invited me over to her house. We chatted long into the night about school and events in our country. By the time we realized how late it was, she suggested that I spend the night as it would be unsafe for me to travel home that late on the train.

When I got to work the next day, my boss was frantic. She said that my father had been calling incessantly from Trinidad all morning, hysterically - demanding to know where I was and what time I was expected in to work. He demanded that I call him as soon as I got in to the office.

Trembling fearfully, I called him. He exploded on the phone. He had called my apartment early the previous evening and there was no answer. He called again and still there was no answer. He kept on calling again and again, but could not reach me. That night, my father slept on the living room floor with the phone by his side, and called my apartment every thirty minutes until the next morning.

He was angry with me because I was out all night, and commanded me to tell him where I was! He then forbade me to ever sleep out ever again. The familiar dread rose up in me.

Although I was twenty-eight years old, I felt that I had to obey him. Daddy's obsession and control over me had a long reach even from Trinidad. He was like an invisible, ominous shadow hovering over me wherever I went. I was always afraid to do or say anything that I knew would make my father angry, even if he was not present at the time.

Chapter 13
Pregnant........and Beaten

During my second year of university, I met and began dating Robert. He seemed like a really wonderful person, and I enjoyed being with him. However, he was not a Christian. Although I knew this relationship was not the Lord's will, I still dated him. I was still looking for someone to fill the void in my life.

I was so enraptured with him and the fact that he liked me, that I did not readily see that he was a volatile and physically abusive man. I lived in fear of me saying and doing the wrong thing, which would in turn elicit his rage.

Robert told me that he and his brother were being evicted from their apartment and had nowhere to live. So I invited them to live with me. I was the only one employed and took care of both him and his brother.

A few months after we began living together, I got pregnant. The prospect of me becoming a mother gave me mixed feelings. I was ashamed that I had sinned against the Lord, but I wanted to have a child. It had always been my heart's desire to get married and have a loving family and home where I felt safe, loved and secure. Maybe now this would be possible, I surmised.

Robert asked me to marry him and I was thrilled. But inside I felt an even bigger void in my heart than I previously had. I felt so lost and far away from the Lord, and that made me feel so unhappy and disgusted with how I was living.

We decided to have a very small wedding. Two weeks before the wedding I pulled together the courage to tell my father about it.

A few days later, he was on a plane heading to New York. A few days before he arrived, Robert beat me ruthlessly because I questioned him about a woman I heard he was seeing. My face and body were battered and bruised. Thankfully, the baby was not harmed by the beating. I later found out that Robert was in a previous relationship where he beat his pregnant girlfriend so badly that she lost the twin babies she was carrying.

When my father arrived, he assessed the situation and took me back to Trinidad. I took a leave of absence from school, as I was determined to complete my education after I had the baby. I was four months pregnant, but I looked more like I was six months. This was due to my having fibroid tumors, which grew as my uterus grew. The doctor I saw in New York had apprised me of the fact that as the fibroids grew, they could suffocate and kill the baby. But I was confident that nothing would happen to my baby.

Immediately after I returned home, Daddy told me that he was taking me to have an abortion. I adamantly refused. "How would you take care of a baby and finish school?" he asked. I suggested that maybe after I had the baby, my mother would take care of it while I went back to university…….to which

Mummy replied "Absolutely Not!" I asked if my sister Leslie would do it. That met with the same the same negative response.

I then decided that I would forego university and stay in Trinidad to take care of my baby. My father told me that I could not stay in their house and that I would get absolutely no support from them if I kept the baby. I felt trapped and did not know what to do. I did not find out until several years later that there was an adoption agency in Trinidad where I could have given up my baby for adoption!

I decided to talk with my aunt, my mother's sister, and get her advice. She had gotten saved and was attending a spirit-filled Church. Aunty Elaine was a gracious spirit-filled Christian who had tremendous wisdom. She said something to me that I never forgot. She said, "Lisa, do not have an abortion. You will regret it. You may never be able to have another child". Nevertheless, I gave in to the pressure from my father to have an abortion.

Daddy drove me to an abortion doctor that he had contacted. Abortion was, and still is, illegal in Trinidad. Therefore, the entire process had to be done covertly. After the procedure, I learned that the baby was a boy. If born, he would have been my parents' only grandson, as my siblings later had only daughters.

I felt such a sense of loss and emptiness in my life because of what I did. I hurt the Lord and my family by what I did. Added to that, I killed my son. I asked the Lord to forgive me, but I felt so much guilt. I could not forgive myself for what I did. It took eight years after the abortion for me to be completely set free.

The uterine fibroids remained enlarged and caused me to develop a heavy monthly flow of blood, and severe anemia. I would have to have surgery immediately to remove the fibroids. It would mean that I would be incapacitated for eight weeks.

When my mother discovered that I would be having surgery, she bought a plane ticket to Maryland so that she would not have to take care of me during my recuperation. My brother's wife, Sonia, was visiting her sister in Canada. So apart from me, the only family members that would be at home were my brother, my father, and his brother, Clyde, who had returned to Trinidad to live. Daddy begged my mother to stay at home to help me, to which she replied caustically, "You take care of her".

The surgery lasted several hours, and the aftermath was very painful. Twelve enormous fibroid tumors were removed from my uterus. I was discharged from the hospital five days after the surgery. The day I got home, one of our neighbors, Mary, came to visit me. Teary eyed, she told me that she could not understand how any mother would leave her daughter in my condition, and not want to take care of her. She said she begged my mother not to go, and pleaded with her to stay and help me. But my mother said bitterly, "She has her father to take care of her". Predictably, when my sister had surgery years later, Mummy cancelled everything and willingly volunteered to take care of her.

Knowing that I was in a lot of pain and unable to walk or stand properly, or to prepare any meals, this very kind neighbor brought me a cooked meal every evening during my incapacitation. This did not include breakfast, as Mary left for work early each day, and was unable to prepare me breakfast. So I had to depend on the men in the house to fix it for me. But they refused. One of them told me that he was too busy to help me. So I was forced to get up from my bed and make my own breakfast. As a result, I developed complications and had to be medically treated.

Before I had the surgery, I met and became good friends with a young woman named Anne Pritchard. She lived on the next block with her mother, siblings and a male relative. My family had become close with theirs while I was away at school. They were all born-again Christians and loved the Lord.

My sister-in-law, Sonia, suggested to me that the Pritchard male relative, Peter, was a nice, gentle, stable Christian, and could be the ideal person for me. Peter and I met and connected well. A few weeks before the surgery, we began a relationship. It was very safe and calming. We conversed about diverse topics. We attended Church together. I visited his family who lived in the country. In short, we had a wonderful time. With the knowledge that I was going back to school soon, he reassured me that he wanted to continue the relationship, and would wait for me until I graduated in a year and a half.

Chapter 14
Et Tu Uncle Simon?

My first challenge in returning to school was to find a place to live. I had to give up my apartment when I took the leave of absence from university to return to Trinidad. The Lord made it possible for me to stay with my mother's cousin and her two young children in their Brooklyn home. This was to be a temporary solution until I found an apartment. My money was almost depleted and I no longer had the job on campus.

A few weeks after I started school, I was offered a job on campus as a College Tutor. I was also accepted into a special university program based on my previous academic performance. Things were going well. But there was still that void in my life. I wanted to have an intimate relationship with the Lord, but just could not seem to. I did not want to just know that He loved me. I wanted to feel it. I wanted Him to be my Daddy. I wanted to have a love relationship with Him. But something was blocking me from having that. And I was still battling depression, guilt, unworthiness and rejection.

I decided to see a Christian psychologist to find out what was wrong with me so that I could be healed from my affliction. I discovered that I had Borderline Personality Disorder, commonly known as BPD. BPD is an emotionally unstable personality disorder characterized by chaotic relationships, impulsive actions, and rapid mood swings. A victim of this disorder has a series of repetitive emotional crises. The person often suffers with dependency, separation anxiety, poor self-image, identity problems, chronic feelings of emptiness and threats of self- inflicted harm such as suicide or self-mutilation. Broken relationships and marriages are often common.

BPD is developed as a result of a very stressful or chaotic childhood, such as physical, emotional and child sexual abuse, abandonment, childhood trauma and violent conflicts. Eating Disorders (usually Bulimia), Mood Disorders, Post-Traumatic Stress Disorder and other Personality Disorders frequently co-occur with BPD. People with Borderline Personality Disorder who have been ill-treated on a recurring basis feel a sense of not belonging, loss of control, low self-esteem and unworthiness. They also have increased stress levels, headaches, depression, chronic illnesses and pain.

Finally, I thought, I was beginning to understand what was wrong with me and why I became that way. But before I could get any help, I had to abandon the therapy because I did not have any money to continue.

Shortly after I stopped the therapy, I moved into the basement apartment in the home of my friend's aunt in Brooklyn. Aunty Jackie and her husband Uncle Simon, as I called them, had three children – two boys and a girl. Their oldest son did not live at home. Their son Ryan and their daughter Stacy were pre-teenagers. Ryan was mentally incapacitated, and did not speak.

Stacy was a troubled girl who suffered with depression and suicidal thoughts. She talked to me a lot about her problems with her father and I prayed with her, counseled her and ministered to her. Stacy longed for the day when she was old enough to move out on her own.

Uncle Simon was an abusive, angry man. Aunty Jackie and the entire household were terrified of him. I had visited Aunty Jackie and Uncle Simon on several occasions before I moved into their home, but evidence of the abuse that took place in their family was not visible then.

Uncle Simon was a very big man with an even bigger voice. He never talked…….he shouted. His powerful voice reverberated throughout the house, and made you want to run and hide so that he would not find you and hurt you. He worked daily, except for Sundays, from 3:00 pm to 11:00 pm. Outside of those hours, he shouted and cursed. He complained about everything; the food tasted nasty, the food was too hot, the food was too cold, the clothes weren't ironed properly, the bed wasn't made up right, or the bed sheets were the wrong color.

He criticized and bad-mouthed everyone he knew, and publicly humiliated and verbally abused them. However, he took the utmost pleasure in verbally and physically abusing Aunty Jackie. She was morbidly terrified of him, and cowered in fear whenever he was present. She was afraid to speak because anything she said was met with anger and aggression. The children were equally petrified of him. Friends and family stopped coming to the house because of him. This man was worse than my father, so I purposefully stayed out of his way.

Aunty Jackie was a wonderful woman, wife and mother. She was a stay at home wife who was an excellent cook and caregiver. She kept the house immaculately clean, and ran the household well. But Uncle Simon was never satisfied with anything she did. She was a very unhappy bruised and battered woman. She cried all the time, and sometimes sat for long hours just staring blankly.

Aunty Jackie loved to listen to the Christian television stations, and became a born-again Christian after listening to a salvation message on TV. She and I got along great and talked and laughed about many things.

Uncle Simon usually came home from work around 12:00 midnight, and always woke up the household. He slammed the door when he came in, which shook the entire house. I could hear his heavy, angry footsteps on the floor above my room in the basement. The profanity that emitted from his mouth was atrocious. Every night we had to endure his tirade of cursing, shouting, and throwing things. Once more I was in living in a dysfunctional home under the threat of violence.

In December that same year, I went home to Trinidad for the Christmas holidays. I looked forward to seeing Peter and his family. Peter picked me up at the airport and drove me home. I noticed that he was very withdrawn and distant with me. I asked him what was wrong ………to which he replied "nothing".

For the duration of my visit, he was very cold and angry with me. I was familiar with this pattern of behavior towards me from every man that liked me. First they would love me, and then they would hate and reject me for no reason. Then they would end the relationship. They themselves could not discern why they behaved that way.

Peter scorned me, mocked me and treated me badly. He attended Christmas functions and refused to take me with him. This was not the Peter I knew. I waited in fear to hear those six little words, "I have something to tell you" followed by why he wanted to end the relationship. I lived in dread that he would speak those words because I could not handle any more rejection. He never spoke them that Christmas.

By the New Year, I left and returned to New York. Life at Aunty Jackie and Uncle Simon's continued the same way I had left it. I thought that if I stayed out of Uncle Simon's line of attack, I would be safe.

I continued working and attending university. I still cried out to the Lord to heal me. I longed for a family of my own – a Christian husband who would love me unconditionally and to become a mother of four or five children. Apart from wanting an intimate relationship with the Lord, all I still really wanted almost all my life was to be part of a warm, loving family and have someone to love and hold me.

Chapter 15

Finding God's Love In The Midst of Abuse and Brokenness

Peter came to New York to visit me a few months after I returned from Trinidad. Aunty Jackie and Uncle Simon allowed him to stay at their home. I realized later that he really did not want to see me, but only needed a place to stay while he was on vacation.

Peter treated me so badly during his visit. He spoke belittling and unkind words to me. His face frequently grimaced in hatred and rage against me. There were times when I thought he would hit me. I could not believe that it was the same Peter that I knew. I knew that he wanted to break up with me and I dreaded it. The old familiar fear of rejection emerged to the surface again. I felt worthless and unloved. I could not bear being rejected any more. It was like my mother rejecting me again and again. The pain was so intense that I felt it throughout every part of my body. It felt like a death. Like a desperate woman, I pleaded and begged with Peter pitifully not to leave me. He said he wouldn't. But then he would start all over again to treat me contemptibly. And I would beg and plead again, and he would relent. This would become an unhealthy cycle for the duration of his visit.

After Peter returned to Trinidad, I became emotionally ill. I planned to go home for the summer vacation and dreaded what would happen when I got there. I cried almost every day. Thankfully my grades did not suffer.

I returned to Trinidad in May. This time Peter did not pick me up at the airport. I saw him the day after I returned, and it was then that he told me that the relationship was over. I was devastated. The sorrow and grief worsened. Most nights I lay in bed awake and crying. I asked God why my life was filled with so much barrenness. But I got no reply.

I still yearned to know the Lord in an intimate way. I wanted to have conversations with Him. I wanted to feel in my heart, and not just know in my head, that He loved me. I wanted to experience Him as my Daddy. I prayed, attended Church and read the Word of God, but I was not experiencing the fruitfulness of the Christian life.

During my previous semester at school, my mother, my siblings and their spouses began attending another Church. I decided to visit. The Church met under a large tent while they awaited the construction of their building. The first Sunday I visited, I was immediately struck by the presence of so many young people. I had never seen so many young people in a Church. They were all colorfully dressed, and came from diverse ethnic backgrounds. There were Caucasians, Chinese, Indians,

Blacks and people of mixed races. They were smiling and greeting each other lovingly. Their faces were alight with the peace and presence of God. Why, I wondered, were so many young people interested in Church?

The Church I previously attended in Trinidad had much fewer young people. In Trinidad, at that time, born-again Christian churches, or "small churches" as they were called did not attract the young. These so called small churches predominantly had older people. Everyone in those Churches dressed in drab colors, mostly white. They seldom smiled or exhibited any vitality which made people feel that God and Church were boring and depressing. The people in these Churches were also mostly of African descent, and also belonged to the lower strata of Society. You seldom saw other ethnic groups or the upper and middle classes attending the born-again Churches. What was the attraction in this Church, I wondered?

As I entered the sanctuary, there were people standing at the entrance who greeted you warmly. The entire ambiance was so welcoming and real. The worship was vibrant and the presence of God permeated the sanctuary. This was so different than what I experienced. And I enjoyed it. The preaching was powerful and dynamic, and I was riveted. At the end of the preaching there was an altar call for those who wanted to be saved and for those who needed healing or had other specific needs. People were at the altar crying and worshipping the Lord as they were being prayed for.

After the service, people greeted each other lovingly, talking and laughing. People I did not know hugged and welcomed me. It was a glorious experience. I decided that I would become a member of this Church.

During a Friday evening service at my new Church, the Pastor preached on the baptism of the Holy Spirit. He taught how the baptism is the overflowing indwelling of the Holy Spirit that the apostles experienced on the day of Pentecost when they became filled with the Holy Spirit and spoke in different tongues. Oh how I wanted that experience. The altar call was made and I went up for prayer but nothing happened.

Later that night when I was at home in bed, I began to pray. Suddenly I was weeping and crying for joy as I experienced the presence of God. I was being baptized in the Holy Spirit! I was no longer praying in English; I was praying in a strange language! Suddenly, as though a dam had split open, I began to worship the Lord and sing in this new language. Oh, what a glorious experience, as I felt the awesome presence of God. I stayed up all night long praying in tongues and worshipping the Lord.

Overnight, my relationship with the Lord had changed. My journey in intimacy with the Lord had begun. I began to have conversations with the Lord, and I heard Him speaking to me. I felt His presence with me more than ever before. I began to worship Him in a way that I had never experienced before. But the road to my healing and deliverance would be long, slow and hard. Although my new Church believed in healing, they did not believe that a Christian could be oppressed by the enemy.... Satan and his demons.

That summer was one of the best times I had ever had. My prayer and worship changed. I was filled with the joy of the Lord. The level of my faith had risen and I knew that the Lord was to be trusted. I also got a summer job at my sister's office where I made friends with several co-workers. All the workers who were employed there that summer were Christians! God had supernaturally done this. What a great time we all had as we shared with each other about the Lord and fellowshipped together.

A few weeks before I was scheduled to return to school, the Lord told me that there was a major problem at Aunty Jackie and Uncle Simon's home, which would make it impossible for me to continue to live there. I immediately called Aunty Jackie. She told me that Uncle Simon had run amok, wielding a gun. He ran through the house screaming and cursing like a demented man, destroying things in his path. He went downstairs into the basement where I lived, and there he did the most damage. He hurled my clothes, books, furniture, telephone and everything in my room into the back yard. He stomped on my things with his massive feet, destroying most of my possessions. I wondered what he would have done to me if I was there. Meanwhile, Aunty Jackie ran out the door and up the street, and Uncle Simon ran after her with the gun. She then ran into a neighbor's house to hide. She waited until he left for work and then came back home. All my possessions were strewn in the back yard, but Uncle Simon forbade anyone to move them. I realized later that the devil was angry with me because I was drawing closer to the Lord. This was backlash and retaliation because of that.

When I heard the account of what Uncle Simon did, I was not perturbed. Instead, I worshipped the Lord. I knew that the Lord would make a way for me to find another place to live. I called a few people before I left, asking them if they knew anywhere I could stay when I returned. But I found nowhere to live.

With my newly found level of faith, I returned to New York, not having anywhere to live, but confident that the Lord had already provided a place for me. I took a taxi from the airport and asked the driver to drop me off at the top of the street that Aunty Jackie lived on.

I waited until Uncle Simon left for work, and then I walked down the street and knocked on the door. I went into the back yard, and gathered up my possessions which were scattered throughout the yard. I packed everything up and asked the next door neighbor if I could leave them at her house until I found a place to live. She agreed. I then went to school and registered for the semester. Since my classes were to begin in two weeks, I decided to take the bus to Maryland to stay with my cousin Diana and her family until school commenced.

As I was about to leave campus, I ran into Marlene who I knew from my former Church in Trinidad. She was looking for a roommate because her brother with whom she shared an apartment was moving out in two weeks. We made arrangements for me to move in with her, and I left for Maryland until it was time for me to come back. God had made a way!

Chapter 16

The Sins of My Father

I graduated from university and returned home to Trinidad where I got a job in the media department of the Prime Minister's office as a TV Director/Producer/Broadcaster. I was living at home with my parents. Nothing had changed. In fact, things had gotten worse. My father continued to have extramarital affairs, many of which were with prostitutes. He had retired from the public service and had received a large cash gratuity which he quickly squandered away on prostitutes and other women.

He developed a gambling problem and placed daily bets on horse racing at off track betting sites. He got a job at a local store to make extra money to supplement his addiction. Daddy continued to control and manipulate me ……and behave obsessively towards me. A co-worker at the store where Daddy worked after his retirement confided to my mother that my father had made sexually explicit remarks to him about me. This resulted in increased verbal and emotional attacks from my mother towards me. I quickly found an apartment to rent in the same building my sister lived, and moved immediately.

One day my father's best friend called me and said he wanted to talk to me. Skeptically, I asked him what it was about.
He told me that he could not discuss it on the phone, and asked if he could come to my apartment. I consented.

Daddy's friend told me, "Your father is a sick man". I asked him what he meant. He said that my father had been seeing a psychiatrist because of his sick, obsessive feelings for me. Daddy described to his friend how he used to sexually abuse me. I was so disgusted and embarrassed that I cried and asked my father's friend to leave my home immediately.

Not long after that incident, my sister and I went to visit our parents. As we approached the house, we saw my parents in the garage along with the police and several other people. My mother and father had a fight and my mother had called the police. There was a lot of commotion in the garage. The neighbors were roused from their houses by the screaming and shouting and the police were trying unsuccessfully to diffuse the situation.

My mother moved out the next day. She packed all her things and moved in with my brother and his wife who had just gotten their own home. Daddy was now left to live alone in the family home. He was helpless. He did not know how to cook, clean or do the laundry. He now had to take care of the household. My sister began preparing his meals which she delivered to him daily. On Sundays he had dinner at my apartment.

In spite of all that I endured, I loved both my parents. I felt so much compassion for my father and prayed that he would become saved and be delivered from the strongholds in his life. On numerous occasions my siblings and I had shared the gospel with him, hoping that he would receive the Lord Jesus Christ as his personal savior. But each time we met with strong opposition.

Daddy angrily insisted that he was perfect and sinless and as he put it, "the only perfect man in the world." We prayed for him diligently for many years that he would become a born- again Christian before he died. I prayed for God's mercy and grace to be upon him, and that God would forgive him for everything he did.

Chapter 17

Still....The Depression

The Church my family and I attended split into three factions. The two Associate Pastors left and started their own churches. All of us, with the exception of my sister, joined one of these splinter churches, which was pastored by Earl Bookman and his wife Joanie. Pastor Bookman and I used to work together many years ago. He used to be decadent and a notorious womanizer. I did not like him very much in those days. But when I returned home from college I met the new man he had become – a godly, warm, compassionate and gentle man of God. I was astounded by the profound transformation.

Because of the intense abuse and rejection I suffered, I did not trust people. I was also still very shy. So for one whole year I silently observed my new pastor and his wife's behavior and their interaction with the sheep before I confided in them about my situation. They were, and still are, true shepherds who are genuine and honest. Their love, patience and kindness, coupled with their servant leadership, have endeared many people to them. They have rescued countless men and women from demonic strongholds.

I grew so much spiritually when I attended my new church. I became a counselor, the audio technician and the assistant children's church director. I drew closer to God and loved to worship Him.

I learned about spiritual warfare and demonic strongholds. At prayer meetings we engaged in spiritual warfare – binding the enemy and tearing down demonic strongholds. I discovered that I had a prophetic gift during one of the prayer meetings. I was sitting next to a young woman when suddenly the Lord began to show me the abuse this woman had suffered from childhood. I began to cry and prophesy to her as the Lord allowed me to feel her pain. She later confirmed that everything the Lord spoke through me was accurate. I was amazed.

That experience was the beginning of so many other prophetic experiences. At first I was uncertain about what was happening. On many occasions I would be at prayer meetings and other ministry meetings when I sensed that the Lord wanted me to prophesy to someone. I was unsure of what I was sensing so I said nothing. But something amazing would happen. I would see two angels walk across the room towards me and gently take me by my arms and walk me over to the person the Lord wanted me to prophesy to. Moved with deep compassion, I would then minister the word of the Lord to the person. Most of the people I prophesied to were abused and hurting women. The Lord allowed me to feel their intense pain, and I would cry as I ministered to them.

I started a ministry at my job. My Christian co-workers and I met at lunch where we worshipped, prayed and shared from the Word of God. The Lord instructed me to have each person in the group take turns each session teaching or preaching. Everyone had the opportunity to be used by God. We met with much opposition from other co-workers, but the group grew and people got saved.

In spite of all this, several things still plagued me. I was heartbroken over aborting my son. The memory of what I did haunted me for eight years. I was also plagued by the lifelong abuse and rejection from my mother, and longed to have a mother-daughter relationship with her.

In college, I unconsciously dismissed her existence so much that I never spoke about her. One day a classmate asked me "Your mother is dead isn't she?' It was then I realized that I had willed myself to stop thinking about her as a means to dealing with the pain. I was also grieved over being sexually abused by my father. For years I tried to discuss with my parents the effect their abuse and rejection had in my life, but they adamantly refused to speak with me about it.

Although my relationship with the Lord had evolved into intimacy, I was still in a lot of emotional pain, and had not yet been delivered from the demonic strongholds of abuse, rejection, and depression. The abuse and rejection was not only from my parents, but also came from family members, friends and acquaintances.

Unknown to my family and friends, I spent most of my life crying. The pain was so horrible at times that my physical body hurt. The attacks of depression were not as frequent as when I was younger, but when they did occur they were unbearable.

Loneliness assailed me and I sometimes felt that I would die. The nightmares were intolerable, and were usually recurring. They were usually about me being raped. I suffered with many physical ailments and had several surgeries, many of which were in the genital area.

One day as I was visiting my brother and his wife, a strange illness swept over me. In the taxi on the way to their house, I suddenly felt as though someone had literally sucked all the air out of my body. My chest and stomach caved in, and visibly looked like a sunken hole. I tried to hold back the tears when I was in the taxi, but the instant I arrived at their house I began to weep uncontrollably. I could not comprehend what was happening to my body.

I rushed into the house begging for help. My family witnessed the hollowness in my chest and stomach, but could not figure out what it was. Neither could the doctors. This strange phenomenon occurred frequently, and was the cause for much concern.

Chapter 18

Mommy Do You Love Me?

I tried to discuss the sexual abuse with my siblings, but they did not want to know about it because they were repulsed by the fact that our father abused me and that my mother resented me. I completely understood their reaction and never held it against them. It was hard for a child to accept that their father was capable of such deviant behavior.

Mummy continued to be hostile and abusive towards me. She still lived with my brother and his wife. Sometimes when I visited her at their home, Mummy prepared meals which other family members partook of in my presence, but I was excluded. I was left out of important family gatherings. She continued to ridicule and berate me openly at every opportunity. She bad-mouthed me with the neighborhood children whom I loved dearly and had great relationships with. I still tried desperately to have a mother-daughter relationship with her, but she still did not want to have one with me.

I was growing very weary with the problem. So I made a decision. I would give the problem a deadline to be resolved. If it was not resolved by that time, I would live with the painful fact that I would never know a mother's love.

On Monday morning I asked the Lord to resolve the problems between my mother and me by midnight on Saturday. I poured out my heart to Him, and told Him that I wanted to have a real relationship with my mother. On Friday, my sister-in-law called me to say that my mother told her, "You do not know what I have endured with Harold and Lisa all these years". She further said that I had been having an affair with my father! Sonia told my mother, "You and Lisa need to meet to talk about the situation". The meeting was set up for Saturday!

That Saturday I entered my brother's house apprehensively but hopefully.....apprehensive as to the outcome of the meeting, but hopeful that at last the problem would be resolved. I went into the kitchen and sat at the table where my mother was already seated. We both sat in an awkward silence, not knowing how to start the conversation.

Finally, I ventured, "Mummy do you believe that I was having an affair with my father? She replied, "Yes". She added that she believed the affair started when I was a child! Then she said that she had hated me all my life because of that. I asked her how she could possibly believe that I would ever have an affair with my father. She sat in stony silence for a few minutes. I reassured her that I would never sleep with my father, and that he had sexually molested me. There was more silence. Then she told me that she was sorry for how she had treated me. I leapt from the chair and threw myself into her arms and bawled. I sobbed loudly "Oh God. I've got a mother! I've finally got a mother!" I was hugging her ....but she was not hugging me! She did not know how to hug me or express her emotions towards me. But I kept on crying from the uttermost parts of my being, "I've got a mother!"

The entire household came running into the kitchen to see what the commotion was all about. My brother, his wife, their daughter Lara, my sister and her two children Dawn and Candace, gathered around us. When they realized what had happened, they all, with the exception of Sonia, went back upstairs to afford us some privacy. Sonia stayed so that she could pray for us. During the prayer, I noticed that the Lord was healing me.

The new found relationship with my mother lasted for one month. After that, she reverted to her old behavior towards me. The grief and the pain gradually set back in. Over the next two months life continued in the same manner. During that time, the Lord began to reveal to Pastor Bookman that Christians could be oppressed by demons and therefore needed deliverance from these spirits. This was, and still is, in many Christian forums, a very controversial subject. Many Christians believe that demonic spirits cannot inhabit a born-again believer. But yet there are many Christians who love the Lord that have had to be delivered from demonic spirits.

Because Christians are in a spiritual war, where we engage demonic spirits daily and are attacked by them, we may need deliverance. The demonic spirits that are oppressing the person must be cast out of them. Often generational curses, which give the enemy legal right to harass the person, must also be broken. Generational curses occur in families where there have been ancestral sins which have produced a curse on successive generations.

In Exodus 34-7, it says "Keeping mercy for thousands, forgiving iniquity and transgression and sin, by no means clearing the guilty, visiting the iniquity of the fathers upon the children and the children's children to the third and the fourth generation. In Lamentations 5:7, it also says; Our fathers have sinned, and are not; and we have borne their iniquities".

Examples of curses include divorce, barrenness, sexual abuse, physical abuse and substance abuse. In order for generational curses to be broken, we have to "number ourselves with the transgressors" as Daniel and other patriarchs did when Israel sinned against the Lord. We have to repent for the sins of our ancestors as though we ourselves have sinned. Daniel 9: 3-9 "Then I set my face toward the Lord God to make request by prayer and supplications, with fasting, sackcloth, and ashes. And I prayed to the LORD my God, and made confession, and said, 'O Lord, great and awesome God, who keeps His covenant and mercy with those who love Him, and with those who keep His commandments, we have sinned and committed iniquity, we have done wickedly and rebelled, even by departing from Your precepts and Your judgments. Neither have we heeded Your servants the prophets, who spoke in Your name to our kings and our princes, to our fathers and all the people of the land. O Lord, righteousness belongs to You, but to us shame of face, as it is this day—to the men of Judah, to the inhabitants of Jerusalem and all Israel, those near and those far off in all the countries to which You have driven them, because of the unfaithfulness which they have committed against You. "O Lord, to us belongs shame of face, to our kings, our princes, and our fathers, because we have sinned against You. To the Lord our God belong mercy and forgiveness, though we have rebelled against Him"

We must then break all resulting curses, and command all the spirits that are attached to the curse to leave.

To be effective, deliverance should always be accompanied by counseling the person being delivered, and the person should be given steps to maintain their deliverance.

I was the first person to receive deliverance at my church. Pastor Bookman and a team, which included my sister-in-law, came to my home to do the deliverance. It took two Saturdays. Each day the session lasted several hours. I was delivered from abuse (including sexual, mental, emotional and physical abuse), rejection, self-rejection, fear of rejection, suicide, abortion, self-hatred and many more demonic strongholds. I wanted them all gone so that I could live in freedom. Any stronghold that the Lord brought to my mind, I told the team so they could deal with them.

In those days, much was not known about deliverance. So the generational curses and word curses were not broken. I also did not know at the time of the occult practices of my grandfather's family, so it was not addressed. Now, however, through experience and more revelation from God, the deliverance ministry at my former church is comprehensive and powerful.

The Lord communicated to me that until I was spiritually and emotionally stronger, I was to discontinue contact with my father. This was to ensure that after the deliverance, the enemy would not try to use him to cause me a setback. I immediately wrote to him and told him that I would be unable to have him over for dinner on Sundays; nor would I be able to communicate with him for a while. He was, of course, greatly offended.

Daddy told my Aunt Elaine and one of his closest friends that I had forbidden him to contact me. Unaware of the circumstances, they were understandably displeased with me. My aunt was the first to call me. In her usual sweet, gentle way she asked me why I forbade my father to come to my house. I told her that it was just for a short period, but could not tell her the reason why. The second person to call was my father's friend, Crystal. She was belligerent. She accused me of being an ungrateful daughter and said that my behavior was not Christ like. I did not tell her what happened. She would not believe me anyway.

Daddy began to write me letters which he slipped under my front door. The letters were those of a man to his lover. He said that he could not live without me, and that if he never saw me again he would die. I was disgusted.

I showed the letters to my Uncle's wife, Glenda, who had returned home to Trinidad to live from England. This was the same aunt who my grandmother told that I, at age 11, was a prostitute. She was appalled. Aunty Glenda was now a wonderful born-again Christian who attended my Church. She apologized to me for believing the lie that my grandmother told her about me.

Because Daddy was banned from my house, he started visiting my church just so he could see me. He pretended to be saved by raising his hands in the air in pretend worship. With upraised hands, he kept looking around to where I sat as if to say "See? I am now a Christian".

When he realized that I was adamant about my decision, he stopped coming to Church. He, however, continued to write me explicit letters which I showed to my sister-in-law and my aunt and then destroyed.

One evening as I waited for Aunty Glenda to pick me up for Church, the Lord showed me that Daddy was going to come to my home that night, camp outside my door and create a scene. I told Aunty Glenda who immediately insisted that I spend the night at her house after the Church service. I found out after that

Daddy did come to my home that night. But I, of course, was not there.

Chapter 19

Early Encounters With God

My job as a TV Director/Producer was very demanding. I often worked six or seven days a week, putting in several hours of work each day. But I loved it immensely.

One day I was speaking to the security guard in the lobby of the building I worked at, when I glanced through the large bay window and saw Jeffrey walking down the street. He did not look like the same person I knew. He was dressed shabbily. His clothes were frayed and threadbare, and he looked bereft. This was not the vibrant, spirit-filled man of God who just by walking into a room commanded the attention of people, young and old.

I walked out onto the sidewalk to speak with him. He was surprised to see me and equally surprised that I would even want to speak to him. We chatted for a while and he invited me out to lunch the next day so we could talk more. I was no longer in love with him. My feelings towards him were now that of a friend.

The following day, at lunch, Jeffrey shared openly with me about his marriage. Shortly after he and his wife married, they built an annex on the lower level of his mother-in-law's house. In the beginning all was well. His wife became pregnant and they had a beautiful daughter. He continued to minister full time, while operating his own business. But insidiously, his wife began to put pressure on him, and he stopped ministering at schools, churches and other establishments. She was not interested in God and ministry and eventually derailed his ministry. She revealed that the father of her child was her boss with whom she had been having a relationship. Added to that, she and her mother destroyed all his clothes, his passport and all his belongings, and ejected him from the house.

He was broken and shattered as though someone had stolen his spirit. His wife divorced him, he was bankrupt, and he no longer had a thriving ministry, nor a business, but worse…….. family and church members spurned him. Many Christians stopped talking to him. To them, he was anathema, someone on whom an ecclesiastical authority has pronounced a ban or curse . I was so hurt by what had happened to him. Since that day, I have prayed for him, at the Lord's leading, for his complete restoration and return to ministry.

Meanwhile, I continued to enjoy a growing intimate relationship with the Lord. There were challenges and relapses as I learned to walk in my deliverance. The years of abuse and rejection had made inroads in my life, and now I had to fight not to succumb to the attacks from the enemy.

At work, the marketplace ministry was growing. I had developed strong relationships with the people in the group, and the times when I was not in studio production were spent giving advice, counseling, praying, and providing support. And I loved it.

I sensed that the Lord was calling me into ministry. By then it had been confirmed that I was called to the office of the prophet. But I sensed that there was more than one thing that the Lord wanted me to do. I sensed that my next step was to migrate to North America. So after inquiring of the Lord and receiving several confirmations, I once again quit my job and moved to Florida.

I lived in Florida for two years, where I became the youth minister at a Church in Ft. Lauderdale. I had given up my desire to marry a wonderful Christian man, and focused on my growing love relationship with the Lord. However, a few months after I arrived, I met Donald, a man who had recently become a member of the Church I attended. A friendship developed followed by a committed relationship. Donald asked me to marry him and I accepted. I was sure that this time it would be different. After all, I had been delivered from all strongholds.

Wedding plans were discussed. Preparations were being made for our marriage. But suddenly, Donald, like all the others before, spurned me. It was like day abruptly turning into night. The sunshine had disappeared in a flash and the darkness dropped in instantaneously. His phone calls became infrequent and he seldom came by to visit. I asked him what was wrong, but he said that everything was okay. I waited in fear to hear those six dreadful words. And they came. He called me and said,

"I have something to tell you." "I do not want to get married". "Why, Lord?", I asked. "Why is this still happening to me?" But there was no response.

The next few months were painful. I continued to seek the Lord for answers but none were forthcoming. At times I became distraught, not only with what happened, but with other major challenging issues. I began to wonder what my purpose was on the earth. Barrenness assailed me as I questioned the reason for my existence. But I held on to the Lord. He became my comfort and my strength.

One evening, as I was on my way home, the old familiar spirit of depression attacked me. I felt that I could not walk the remaining few yards to my apartment. Suddenly I saw two large angels come and gently take me by each hand and walk me up the street. It was a glorious experience.

Chapter 20

Miracles From Heaven

In 1992, I migrated to Canada. Canada was where I really wanted to live. I had visited Toronto in the early 1970s and loved it. I had applied for Canadian residence before I left Trinidad, and it was finally approved. I moved to Toronto in February.

My friend, Beverly, who I knew from Trinidad, lived in Toronto, but I did not know what area in Toronto she lived. I felt that there was a specific reason for me to find her. I asked the Lord to supernaturally allow me to find her. The same week I migrated, I went to a flea market down the street from where I lived. There, shopping at the flea market was Beverly! We hugged excitedly. Beverly invited me to visit her Church which was very close to my house.

That Sunday, as I walked into the Church, I was elated to find that many of the Church members were Christians I knew from Trinidad. Some of them were from the Trinidad IVCF group I used to belong to. I felt that I had come home, so to speak.

I became a member of the church, joined the choir and became actively involved in the ministry. I became part of a wonderful group of Christians. I got an accounting job, albeit a temporary one, at a major corporation. I moved into a beautiful basement apartment in the home of a European family. My relationship with the Lord was becoming increasingly more intimate. Summarily, all was well.

I experienced so many divine miracles when I lived in Canada. I woke up one morning with a pain in my chest. I felt weak and had trouble breathing. Nevertheless, I got dressed and went to work. While at work, the pain in my chest grew worse and now spread down my left arm. Both my shoulders hurt. I could not raise either of my arms. I also did not have the strength to breathe air through my nostrils. Weakness invaded my entire body.

A co-worker encouraged me to go to the doctor. I decided to go after work. Since I was new to Toronto, I did not yet have a personal doctor. So I looked through the yellow pages of the phone book to find one. But because I was not familiar with the city, I was unable to tell from the listings where any of the doctors' offices were located. I did not know their proximity to my job or home, nor did I know how many buses I would have to take to get there. As I glanced through the phone book, a doctor's name became illuminated in my spirit. I called to book an appointment, and was given one for 6:00 pm that evening. It turned out that the doctor's office was around the corner from my house! I knew that it was the Lord's handiwork.

I made it home, painfully, from work, and left my house a few minutes before 6:00 pm for my visit to the doctor. I could barely walk down the street. It was a long, laborious walk, and I had to stop to rest and breathe every few minutes. Finally, I reached the doctor's office. He examined me and found nothing wrong with me. As I got up to leave, he suddenly said that he wanted to give me a blood test. There was a lab in the same building, so I went there to do the test. Although the lab was about to be closed for the day, they drew my blood and said that the test results would be available in a few days. I took a taxi back to my apartment and went to bed.

That evening about 8:30 pm, the phone rang. It was the doctor. He sounded very alarmed. The lab decided to test my blood right after I left, and called the doctor immediately.

My hemoglobin count was dangerously low. The hemoglobin count measures the ability of your red blood cells to carry oxygen. A normal hemoglobin count is 12-16 for women. My hemoglobin count was 5! At this level I was subject to heart failure or a stroke. The pains in my chest, shoulders and arms, and the debilitating weakness and inability to breathe were signs of the onset of a stroke or heart failure. The low hemoglobin count was caused by excessive menstrual bleeding. The fibroids had grown back, causing me to bleed excessively each month.

The doctor expressed that people with a hemoglobin count of 5 could not even walk, and marveled that I was able to walk and function for so long. He further said that when the lab called him with the results he was at his home which was over an hour from his office, and therefore could not get back to his office in time to find my phone number to call me. He knew that I had to get to the hospital immediately to have a blood transfusion or I could die. But he did not know my phone number. Suddenly, he said, my phone number flashed before his eyes! He said he was not a religious man or a praying man, but he knew that it had to be God who did that! I spent several days in the hospital during which time I received blood transfusions and became stabilized.

Chapter 21
The Presence of God

My first winter in Canada was the country's fiercest winter in 75 years. It was brutally cold. Although I only had one block to walk when I came off the bus each day from work, it felt like it took a long time to get home. My ears, fingers and toes felt like they would fall off. It was also fiercely cold in my apartment. The landlord refused to put on the furnace, and used only his fireplace to heat the entire house. This was a huge house and I lived in the basement, so I felt the harsh effects of the cold.

While at home, I wore two sets of pajamas, thermal underwear, two pairs of socks, gloves, a wool cap, earmuffs and my thick winter coat. But I was still cold. At night I slept under two comforters in the same garb. I complained to the landlord about the situation, but he refused to do anything about it.

It snowed almost every day. There was always ice on the ground. One day as I left my home, the ground was so encased with ice that I feared that if I stepped on it I would fall. Suddenly I heard the Lord begin to speak to me. He guided me as I walked, telling me exactly what part of the ice to place my feet on so that I would not fall! He would say "go right", "go left" or "stop". With the Lord's loving help, I did not fall or slip!

Some of my greatest experiences with the Lord were in Toronto. At the end of my temporary job, I could not find another job. So while I was waiting, I stayed at home and spent hours and hours in the Word of God, worship and prayer. I got up early, had breakfast and a shower and went back to bed, the only place that was warmer than the horribly cold apartment, and spent intimate times with the Lord. Oh, how wonderful it was. I knew and experienced the Father's love. I knew in my heart, and not just in my head, that He loved me. And I loved Him so much!

I received revelations from the Lord and He spoke to me about so many things. The times of worship ushered in His glorious presence. Sometimes I worshipped and prayed all day or all night long. Then something amazing happened. My spirit began to pray and worship all day and all night. I heard these wonderful songs being sung in my spirit and prayers going forth from me involuntarily. My mouth did not sing or pray. My spirit did. I could not turn it off! Even when I was speaking to someone, I heard it. When I was on the bus I heard it. It went on for weeks. It reminded me of the word in 1 Thessalonians 5: 17 which says "pray without ceasing".

The presence of God that was ushered into my life during that time was divine. I neither wanted nor needed a husband because I did not want anyone to disrupt my relationship with the Lord. I did not need a man to validate me or make me feel worthy. I felt complete in the Lord. God had filled the void in my life.

In December that year, an older woman at my Church asked me to accompany her to a Christian conference in California. This annual conference was held by a well-known ministry in the United States. I was very excited about attending.

There were thousands of people from all over the United States and other countries. The atmosphere was charged with the awesome presence of God. Two days before the conference ended, I sat next to two ministers from California. We chatted amicably. I felt drawn to the younger of the two.

On the final day of the conference, although unplanned, the two ministers ended up sitting next to me again. For the first part of the service, they were sitting somewhere else, but after the anointing segment they had to move to another part of the auditorium, as their previous seats were now occupied. They happened to sit in the same row I sat. At first they did not realize that they were sitting next to me, but when they did, the younger of the two, Brian, seemed surprised to see me again.

He greeted me and we chatted for a while. A few minutes of silence elapsed before Brian spoke again. He boldly said that the Lord told him that I was his wife! We exchanged phone numbers and addresses, and he promised to contact me.

The day after I returned to Toronto, there was a phone call from Brian. What ensued was a long distance relationship filled with phone calls and letters. Brian wrote me a letter each day, telling me all about himself. He wrote that he was a gentle and tender man who loved the Lord with his whole heart. He loved to take long walks, and loved nature and animals. He said he also loved children and wanted to have some of his own when he married.

Brian was a native Californian, and had two siblings. He said he had gotten saved when he was a child, but had fallen away from the Lord when he was eighteen. Before he rededicated His life to the Lord, he had spent most of his adult years drinking, using drugs, and womanizing. When he came back to the Lord, he quit his lucrative job, sold his five bedroom home, and bought a 40 foot motor home. A motor home is a motor vehicle with facilities for cooking, living and sleeping.

He drove his motor home to a desolate rural town where he had bought several acres of land on a mountain. Brian lived on his mountainous property in his motor home for three years. His purpose was to be alone with the Lord, to commune with Him and study the Bible. There was no water, no electricity, nor any people around for several miles. It was just Brian and his two dogs, Sam and Luke.

A few months before we met, an Associate Pastor from the neighboring town of Williamsville asked Brian to move there because she wanted him to attend her Church. He did. He drove his motor home into the town and parked it on the property of a couple from the Church. He lived there in his motor home.

Brian asked me to marry him, and I accepted. We planned to live in Williamsville in his motor home. Our plans included ministering together and having children. But just before I left for California, an unforeseen change in our circumstances forced us to get married in Toronto. Since I had already given notice on my apartment, I now had to stay with a Christian couple while the wedding was being planned.

Ours was a very small wedding with less than twenty people in attendance. Brian and his mother, Susan, arrived in Toronto a few days before the wedding. His father, Paul, was unable to come. The ceremony went well.

We spent our honeymoon at a hotel in Toronto. On our wedding night, Brian changed into another person. The transformation resembled that of Jekyll and Hyde. His behavior was bizarre. When three thumping sounds came from the occupants of the room above us, Brian claimed that it was God trying to get his attention. He said that God was angry with him because he was in bed with his wife!

He jumped off the bed, fell on his knees and asked God to forgive him! At first I thought he was joking, but when I realized that he was serious, I became stupefied. He jumped back into the bed and with a glazed look in his eyes, he said, "Everything I told you about me is a lie!" He added, "I will be so sorry for you when you get to Williamsville." He also said that he lied about wanting to have children.

I felt like I was the main character in a horror movie. Maybe, I thought, there was a hidden camera somewhere. But there wasn't. What was happening was real. People told me afterwards that I should have walked away from the marriage that night, but I took my vows very seriously and wanted to make the marriage work.

The next day, we returned to my friends' home. At breakfast, Brian was sullen and angry. I asked him what was wrong, but he refused to reply. Each attempt I made to converse with him met with rigid silence. I wondered what I had done to displease him. Suddenly, he spoke. " Why didn't you pass me the butter?", he asked. I told him that he never asked me to pass the butter. He looked at me with dead eyes and said, "I told God to tell you to pass me the butter and you did not. Why?" Bewildered, I asked him, "Why didn't you just ask me for the butter? Isn't it silly to ask God to ask me to pass the butter when you could ask me yourself?'" "No", he said. "I am on a word fast………I am fasting my words, so I cannot talk to anyone!" I realized then that there was something terribly wrong with him, but the true extent of what it was would soon be realized.

Chapter 22

Deliver Me From Evil

Brian returned to California three days after our wedding. I had to wait in Canada for my application for US residency to be approved. It would take a couple of months to be granted. As soon as Brian left, I became very ill. I was very anemic, due to the fibroids, and thus was extremely weak and tired all the time. Sometimes I could not even get out of bed in the morning.

A week after Brian left, the Christian couple I was living with evicted me from their home because as they put it " we do not want to have to deal with your situation". So I moved to the home of another Christian couple, Tom and Lila.

While I was at Tom and Lila's home, I was offered a baby-sitting job by Lila's cousin Donna. The agreement was that I would babysit Donna and her husband's one year old daughter, Tasha, every day while they were at work. Tom and Lila, in conjunction with Donna and her husband, decided that they would bring Tasha to Tom and Lila's home daily where I would babysit her.

It was so wonderful taking care of Tasha. She was an exuberant, playful child and at times quite challenging to take care of, but I loved it.

A few days after I moved in with Tom and Lila, I began to experience tremendous spiritual warfare. I had never experienced such intense spiritual attacks like this before. I cannot adequately convey in words the intensity of the attack. It felt like Satan and every demonic spirit that exists had launched a unified attack against me. I thought that I was losing my mind. Thoughts of death, suicide and confusion flooded over me. Spirits of fear gripped me, and an unusual fatigue overwhelmed me. At times I had difficulty breathing.

I was being tormented day and night, but it was worse at night. I could not sleep. The atmosphere in my bedroom was saturated with a sickly, evil presence. When I turned the lights off, I could see hundreds of grisly yellow eyes in the room watching me. I bound and cast out demonic spirits. I prayed and worshipped the Lord. I read scripture. But the attacks and the satanic manifestations did not cease. I could not understand where the attacks were coming from. I did not tell anyone what was happening because I did not think they would believe me.

One night, as I lay in bed, I glanced up at the mirror and saw something strange. Looking at me in the mirror was a man and a woman! I thought that I was becoming crazy. How could I possibly be seeing people looking at me in a mirror? Surely I must really be losing my mind. But when I looked again…….there they were. I did not understand what was happening to me, or why.

In the midst of this horrible attack, I discovered that I was pregnant. Now, added to the tormenting attacks, I was sick all day long. But shortly after the pregnancy diagnosis, I miscarried. Tom and Lila and their pastor Earl and his wife, who I knew from Trinidad, rallied around me and supported me. Earl immediately called Brian to tell him what had happened. Brian nonchalantly said, "So what?" Under duress from Earl, Brian flew to Toronto two days later and stayed with me for a week.

When Brian saw me he was appalled to see how distraught I looked. I had lost a lot of weight. My skin looked pallid, and there were dark circles under my eyes. I explained to him what I was dealing with, but he was very unsympathetic. He kept saying that I was not the woman he met, and that I looked different. He looked at me scornfully.

Brian brought a publication from his Church which listed the names of church members along with their photographs. As I browsed through the photographs I made a staggering discovery. The Associate Pastor and her husband were the same couple I saw in the mirror in my bedroom!

On the last day of Brian's visit, I prayed and asked the Lord to show me where the spiritual attacks were coming from. I asked Him to reveal it to me by midnight that night.

Brian and I went to bed early that night. We chatted for a while. But at 11:45 pm, Brian said that he had something to tell me. I asked him what it was, and he said that a young man in his church identified someone in the church who was a witch. Apparently, this young man had been in prayer when the Lord revealed it to him. I asked Brian who was the person the young man identified as the witch. But the moment I asked that question, Brian fell into a stupor. I shook him out of it, and asked him the same question. He replied, "It was………", Before he could utter her name, he fell into another stupor. This became a pattern. I would ask him who it was…….he would try to say the person's name, but would fall into a stupor. By this time I realized that it was the enemy, so I began to pray and bind the demonic spirits that were trying to keep him from telling me who it was. Finally, he told me that the person was the Associate Pastor! This was the same Associate Pastor, who, along with her husband, manifested in the mirror in my bedroom!

The young man, who was a dedicated Christian, told the Senior Pastor of the Church that the Lord showed him that the Associate Pastor was a witch. He did not believe him. Instead, the Senior Pastor told the Associate Pastor what he said. Immediately after that, this young man went raving mad, and had to be institutionalized.

Brian also told me that periodically, other people warned the Senior Pastor that the Associate Pastor was a witch, but he never believed it. Once a pastor came to minister at the Church, and when he met the Associate Pastor, he told the Senior Pastor that she was a witch. He did not believe him. Anyone who exposed this woman ended up becoming insane.

Brian also revealed to me that this Associate Pastor told the Church that the Lord instructed her to pray over everyone to receive what she called "the burning spirit". According to Brian, this "burning spirit", was the Holy Spirit! He said the Associate Pastor claimed that the "burning spirit" exposed and burned up the sins in people's lives whether or not they wanted it to happen. She imparted this spirit, by the laying on of hands, to people. Sometimes, Brian claimed, she would go into other churches and establishments and release this "burning spirit" into people's lives. According to Brian, everyone who received the "burning spirit" experienced tremendous torment, confusion and trouble. But, Brian insisted, this was only the Holy Spirit at work in people's lives in order to bring them into holiness.

I explained to Brian that the Holy Spirit does not operate in that manner. The Holy Spirit is gentle and does not force Himself on anyone. He also does not release torment and confusion in the lives of Christians. I explained to him that the "burning spirit" is really a demonic spirit. But, Brian said I was wrong.

He told me that the first time he met the Associate Pastor, she laid hands on him and released the "burning spirit" into his life. He also played a tape for me to listen to where the Associate Pastor confirmed what Brian told me. On that tape, she could be heard praying over Brian as she laid hands on him to receive a greater measure of the "burning spirit". She also gave him what she called "the power of command". The "power of command" gave Brian the power to command the "burning spirit" to every person he came into contact with........whether they wanted it or not. She also prayed, "I send the burning spirit to Canada to be released to Lisa!"

Now I knew exactly where the spiritual attack was coming from. I told Brian that I had asked God to show me, by midnight that night, where the spiritual attack emanated from. He realized then that what he told me about the witch and the "burning spirit" was God revealing the truth to me.

Brian made me vow that we would not tell anyone what happened that night. Instead, he said that we should pray about the situation, and ask God for further confirmation. I agreed. Something as serious as this warranted confirmation, as I did not want to believe something like this about any pastor. What if we were wrong? We also realized the danger to both of us if the Associate Pastor knew that we suspected she was really a witch.

Brian returned to California the next day while I stayed in Toronto awaiting the approval of my US permanent residency. The spiritual attacks against me intensified. The spiritual warfare that I had learned at my former church in Trinidad was powerful, but it did not seem to be effective against the spirits of witchcraft that were trying to destroy me.

The Lord instructed me that I should use the weapon of praise and worship against the enemy. Satan hates praise and worship primarily because when we worship, the Lord inhabits (dwells in) our praises. When we worship, the enemy flees.

I spent hours each day and night praising and worshipping the Lord. I felt nothing. Normally when I worshipped, I would experience the glorious presence of God. But I felt absolutely nothing. It was as if the heavens were brass. That is, it felt like the Lord was not present.

But in obedience to the Lord, I continued to worship every day for weeks until I felt the change in the spiritual atmosphere. Then things began to happen. My application for permanent residency, which was hitherto taking extremely long to be processed, was approved. I would be leaving Canada in one week to live in California.

With only one week before I left Canada, Tom and Lila evicted me from their house. I had nowhere to go. I reminded them that I was leaving in one week and asked them if they would let me stay until that time. But they said no, and that I must leave that same day. I would also not be able to baby-sit Tasha at their house. I really needed the money.

I spoke with Donna about the problem and suggested to her that I baby sit Tasha at her house instead. She said that Tom and Lila told her that I quit the job! I was very hurt and perplexed by what they did. I now had no job and nowhere to live. So on one of the coldest days of winter, I packed my things and left. I walked down the street, not knowing where to go. I was physically weak and still suffering with anemia. I trudged along the street wearily. I got to a pay phone and called a friend who told me that I could spend the night at her house. She lived very far away. I had to take a train and two buses to get to her town, and then walk for several blocks to get to her house. The journey was long and tiring, as I struggled with extreme physical weariness.

I spent one night at her house, and then moved in with another family for my last week in Canada. I moved to California on the Saturday of that week.

Many people, who I told my story to years later, asked me why I stayed married to Brian. Why, they asked, did I still go to Williamsville to live? The short answer was that I did not want to break my wedding vows. I also felt that I needed to pray for my husband to be delivered. But, Brian did not want to be delivered. So I spent five years in a highly abusive marriage and simultaneously endured relentless personal attacks by witches and Satanists who lived in Williamsville.

Chapter 23
Back In The Fire

The exact moment I arrived in Williamsville, I sensed the heaviness and darkness over the town. The place was barren and looked like an old abandoned town in a western movie. It felt as though evil forces had drained all the life out of the town. People seldom walked along the streets. Williamsville was virtually a wilderness.

This small rural town, at the time I lived there, had a population of approximately three thousand people. The populace, which was predominantly white, had about 0.5 % African Americans. Over half the population of the town practiced witchcraft. The Satanists and witches boasted that they controlled the town. Of course, I did not know all this when I first arrived.

The night I arrived in Williamsville, Brian introduced me to the Collins on whose property the motor home was parked. The Collins' house was just a few yards from the motor home. I instantly bonded with Helen Collins who was having major marital problems. Her husband Jerry seemed strange. We chatted for a while, and then Brian and I went to the motor home.

The motor home was smaller than I thought. The living area, kitchen and bedroom were minute, but the bathroom was even smaller.

The electricity was being supplied by a cable which ran from the Collins' home to ours. There was no heat, and because the town was located in Northern California, it was very cold.

After settling in, I went to take a shower. I was in the shower for about 2 minutes, and had just lathered my skin with soap, when suddenly the water was turned off. I called out to Brian to tell him what happened, and he said that he had turned off the water because he was teaching me how to take short showers! He refused to turn the water back on so I had to go to bed with soap lather on my skin.

The next day, Brian took me to the home of the Associate Pastor and her husband. The Associate Pastor and her husband seemed like really nice people. But that was a façade for who they really were. She told me that when Brian returned from Toronto, he told them that I said she was a witch! Brian told them everything that had transpired the night before he left Canada! I was petrified. How could he do that, I wondered? He not only broke our promise not to tell anyone, but he also exposed me to grave danger.

Brian was a violently abusive man, physically, mentally and emotionally, whom I could not trust. He shared everything that I did or told him to the Associate Pastor, his mother and everyone he could tell. And he usually embellished the facts. He frequently lied outright about me, discrediting me in other people's eyes. He controlled everything I said or did. I became afraid to do or say anything.

His way of reasoning, and behaving was abnormal. He was, I discovered, very cruel and very demonized. I felt so isolated and afraid because I was so very far away from my family and friends.

The first week I arrived, as we were getting ready for Church, I tried to locate an iron to press my clothes. I couldn't find one so I asked him where it was. He said that he did not have one and that I should wear my clothes rumpled because as he put it "Jesus is coming back soon, so we shouldn't be bothered with such vanity"!

Brian ministered at the jail in Williamsville and at a prison in the mountains. I accompanied him to the prison the week after I arrived. The road to the mountains was narrow and winding. There was a sheer drop on each side of the road. On the way back from the prison, Brian told me that he wanted us to spend the night on his wilderness mountain property where he used to live. I did not feel comfortable doing so because of the intense witchcraft that blanketed the area. The entire area was infested with covens of witches. There was also no water or electricity, and we would have to sleep in his pick-up truck. Added to that, I was exhausted and sick and wanted to get home.

Brian was angry with me because I did not want to go. He pretended to get sleepy, and asked me to talk to him so he would not fall asleep at the wheel. I had only talked with him for about five minutes when he commanded me to shut up. He forbade me to talk any further. Then he began to pretend that he was falling asleep. He kept driving the car close to the edge of the road. We were precariously close to tumbling down the side of the mountain. I was so terrified, but he would not stop. He drove like an intoxicated man, meandering all over the road, and veering close to the precipice. I kept talking loudly, trying to keep him awake, not knowing that he was doing it on purpose.

As soon as we got home, Brian instantly became alert. All "sleep" had left him. He said he had some things to do, so I went to bed. I woke up around midnight and realized that he had gone. He left a note on the table saying, "Nobody tells me what to do. If I want to spend the night in the mountains, I will. I have gone back to the mountains, and I will be there for a few days. I have taken Sam with me". Sam was his dog. His other dog, Luke, died a few weeks before I arrived. Brian buried Luke with a Bible in his paw!

Brian stayed in the mountains for five days. He left me with no groceries and no money. The only thing in the motor-home to eat was a pack of black eyed peas. I cooked it and ate it for the five days he was gone.

Brian's mother, Susan, called while he was gone. We did not have a phone in the motor home so she called at the Collins' home. I told her that Brian was not home, but I did not want to tell her what he did. But, realizing that something was wrong, she asked me if everything was okay. I did not want to tell her, but she insisted. She assured me that she would keep what I told her confidential. So I told her. She was very displeased with Brian.

Later that week, we drove to Brian's parents' house in San Francisco which was about three hours from Williamsville. Susan told Brian and I that she wanted to speak with us. She told him what I had confidentially shared with her about Brian. She now defended her son's actions and spoke to me nastily. I sat in painful silence while she said that she was positive that I was a disappointment to my family. Brian gave me a murderous look. I did not know how he would retaliate against me.

I finally met Brian's father, Paul, who had been unable to attend the wedding in Toronto. Paul was a very abusive husband and father. My mother-in-law Susan always looked very sad and oppressed all the time. He verbally abused her, his children, his daughters-in-law, his grandchildren............and everyone else. They were all afraid of him. He was also very manipulative and controlling. Susan could not do or say anything unless he approved. And he usually did not. Susan, like so many other women, was so abused that she believed that the abuse was normal. She suffered greatly for many years.

Paul's behavior was obsessive. The jars in the cabinet had to be lined up perfectly or he would explode in anger. Things had to be done his way, or no way at all, or else he would go berserk.

Paul did not like me. Whenever we visited them, he would seem nice for the first day, but after that he was sullen and unkind towards me. Once I went into the refrigerator to get a can of soda. I took a glass and put ice in it. As I was about to pour the soda into the glass, Paul came into the kitchen, grabbed the glass from me and threw the ice into the sink angrily. "You don't need any ice", he said. "The soda is already cold"

I discerned that there were demonic spirits in my father-in-law that hated me. There was so much tension in the house when we visited my in-laws. I could sense the hatred from the demonic spirits being projected towards me. Even Brian sensed it.

Chapter 24

Battered Wife

During the five years I lived in Williamsville, I was under immense attack from the enemy, particularly from spirits of witchcraft. The anointing attracts attack from the enemy. The enemy sensed the anointing on my life, and launched a brutal attack against me which made the attacks I had experienced in Canada seem tame by comparison. I was tormented day and night by spirits of witchcraft, death, insanity, fear and a host of other demonic spirits.

Jerry Collins, on whose property we lived, became violently angry with Brian and me. Jerry, a known molester of children, was appointed to the position of Youth Minister by the Associate Pastor! Brian protested to the Associate Pastor that it was wrong to have a child molester in charge of the Junior Church. She told Jerry what Brian said and Jerry became angry with us. Jerry was also angry because he found out that I had ministered to his wife about the abuses she suffered from him.

One night, Jerry came to the motor home and threatened to kill me. His face contorted with rage as he spoke. There was so much evil being emitted from him, that it was terrifying. Later that night, he loaded his gun and shot at me through the window. I threw myself on the floor before the bullets could hit me. The second round of bullets hit the side of the motor home. The next night, while we were out, Jerry rigged the motor-home to explode when we turned on the lights. The Lord revealed the plot, and we escaped death.

Although our lives were in danger, Brian refused to move from the Collins' property! He said he was not afraid of Jerry and would not allow him to move us off his property. I pointed out that it was Jerry Collins property and not ours! Our lives were threatened, but that did not concern Brian. I begged him to move, but he refused to do so.

Finally, Carl and Tiffany , a couple from the church invited us to live on their property. Carl was the Associate Pastor's son. His wife, Tiffany, took special interest in me. She befriended me and chatted with me every day.

The spiritual attacks against me intensified. I had to be alert day and night. I spent each day, for five years in extreme spiritual warfare and praise and worship. I felt that my life depended on it. Demonic spirits manifested in the motor home daily. I was bombarded by the enemy twenty-four hours of the day. It was like living in hell.

Brian and I were having many problems in our marriage. The Associate Pastor told Brian that he and I needed marital counseling. She counseled us separately, but never as a couple. She told me that I should stay away from Brian, and told me to divorce him. She said that Brian and I should live apart so that God could restore the marriage. She counseled many other couples in the same manner. As a result, there were many couples in the church who lived apart from each other.

The church members never read their bibles, and depended solely on the word preached from the pulpit. When I shared with some of them the importance of reading their bibles, they were annoyed with me and said that they did not need to read their bibles because they got the word from the pastor.

Several women in the church, after they had received the "burning spirit", had become oppressed by demonic spirits. They confronted the Associate Pastor about what they were experiencing.

Her reply to them was, " the Lord has emptied you of demonic spirits and is waiting to fill you back up". That doctrine is contrary to the Word of God. It is vital to keep your spiritual temple filled with the Holy Spirit especially after deliverance. If not, you will be open to demonic infestation.

In Luke 11:24-26 it says: "When an unclean spirit goes out of a man, he goes through dry places, seeking rest; and finding none, he says, 'I will return to my house from which I came.' And when he comes, he finds it swept and put in order. Then he goes and takes with him seven other spirits more wicked than himself, and they enter and dwell there; and the last state of that man is worse than the first."

One day I received a phone call from the Associate Pastor. I was at the time still questioning whether or not she was a witch because she was so friendly. She called to give me an assignment.

The assignment was for me and her daughter-in-law, Tiffany, to minister to another member of the church. She said that this church member, Rose, was a former witch who apparently had gotten saved. Rose's daughter, Toni, was still a witch, but wanted to get out of the craft. Toni had recently gotten pregnant and did not want her child to be subject to witchcraft. Toni, however, was not saved. The witches threatened to kill Toni's unborn child. Rose's life was also threatened.

The Associate Pastor wanted Tiffany and I to pray with Rose. I found it very strange that a problem of this magnitude would be assigned to only two people. More people should have been involved in intercessory prayer and spiritual warfare for Rose and her daughter. I realized later that the assignment was a ruse to expose me to more attacks from the witches in the area.

I met with Rose who revealed a lot to me about the witchcraft in Williamsville. She said that the witches and Satanists in Williamsville boasted that they controlled the town. Rose also revealed that there were several covens in Williamsville, and that on special occasions the witches often met at the cemetery. There was a special tomb which could be pulled back to reveal a tunnel. The witches enter through this tunnel which runs all the way to Mt. Shasta where they perform their rituals.

Mt. Shasta is located about 60 miles south of the California-Oregon border and 77 miles north of Redding, California. It is known for its mysticism and tremendous beauty. The area's Native Americans revere it as the center of creation. They believe that the "Great Spirit" created Mt. Shasta by pushing down snow and ice through a hole from heaven, and then used the mountain to step onto the earth. According to the native Americans, when the Great Spirit stepped onto the earth, he created the trees, the animals, the birds, the fish and the rivers and streams.

Today, descendants of the Native American tribes who still live in the Mt. Shasta area perform ancient rituals in honor of the mountain. Each year, they invoke the mountain's spirit with ritualistic dances that are supposed to ensure the continual flow of the sacred springs.

Witches, Satanists and New Age followers believe that the mountain has mystical power. They believe that it is a sacred source of harmony.

Various new age groups believe that Mt. Shasta is one of the Seven Sacred Mountains of the World, a landing spot for UFOs, a cosmic power point, and that it has magic crystals. Rosicrucians, a secret mystical society , believe that Mt. Shasta is the dwelling place of the Lemurians. They claim that these Lemurians are a race of spiritually advanced super-humans who can transform themselves from the physical state to the spiritual state at their own wills. The Rosicrucians claim that these super-humans are tall, graceful and supple, and have much larger heads than the average human. Their power is believed to be enhanced by magic crystals they brought to Mt. Shasta when they escaped from Lemuria, their native home. Lemuria, they claim, is a lost continent off the Pacific coast which was destroyed by the eruption of a volcano.

Other occult groups believe that it is the home of the ascended masters which they believe are spiritually advanced beings that manifest "the luminous essence of divine love" and assist human evolution. These ascended masters are really demonic spirits.

Mt. Shasta is also home to several New Age study centers where people explore mystical teachings concerning the mountain. Essentially, Mt Shasta is a seat of evil where Satanists, witches, new agers and secret societies practice witchcraft, mysticism and the occult.

Rose disclosed that it was in the underground tunnels leading to Mt. Shasta and at the mountain itself where covens of witches in Williamsville met. Rose herself was being threatened by these witches that if her daughter Toni left the coven, they would not only kill her unborn baby but Rose as well.

When I told Brian what Rose revealed, he wanted me to go to the cemetery with him late at night and confront the witches! I declined. He told me that I was a coward!

I refused to meet with Rose when I realized that it was a setup to destroy me. I wanted Brian and myself to leave Williamsville immediately. I begged him to leave, but he snarled at me and said, "You go if you want. I am staying here". I prayed daily for

God to open his eyes to what was happening, but he stubbornly refused to acknowledge what was taking place. So I returned to Trinidad alone for a few weeks. I needed help. I was growing weak, physically, mentally, emotionally and spiritually. I had to get away to re-fortify myself and get deliverance from the strongholds.

I stayed in Trinidad for three weeks. I told my former pastor about the situation. He prayed with me and ministered deliverance to me. During the deliverance, the Lord revealed to Pastor Bookman that the Associate Pastor was really a high priestess. The Lord also showed him that she was an angel of light.

Angels of Light are described in the Bible in 2 Corinthians 11:13-15: "For such are false apostles, deceitful workers, transforming themselves into apostles of Christ. And no wonder! For Satan himself transforms himself into an angel of light. Therefore, it is no great thing if his ministers also transform themselves into ministers of righteousness, whose end will be according to their works"

These angels of light.....witches and satanists..... infiltrate Christian churches to destroy them from within. Such was the case with this pastor. However, I would soon discover that there was more than one witch at that church.

Pastor Bookman broke spells, spirits of witchcraft and black magic which were placed on me by the Associate Pastor and which also transferred to me through sex with Brian. When the

Associate Pastor's name was mentioned, the demonic spirits manifested violently. These spirits said that she had much power. The 'burning spirit" which she had imparted into Brian's life was the way that she kept him and others under her control. She also used the "burning spirit" to get information from people. That explained why Brian reported everything that happened in our lives to her. Pastor Bookman urged me to leave Williamsville immediately. He said that we were in Satan's territory and could be destroyed.

A few days after the deliverance, Sonia and I prayed together about the situation. The Lord showed her a woman with long blonde hair casting spells over Brian and me. This woman was not the Associate Pastor, but a younger woman. It was revealed that this woman wanted Brian to be a warlock. She, and the other witches, saw me as a threat, and wanted me out of the way so they could get to Brian. They also wanted me destroyed because of the ministry call on my life.

At a meeting at my former church in Trinidad, Pastor Bookman preached about fulfilling the call to ministry. He invited to come to the altar, those who wanted to commit to the Lord that they would fulfill their call, regardless of the price and the trials and tribulations that came with it. The anointing of the Holy Spirit fell upon me powerfully. I knew that the Lord was calling me to fulfill a greater work in the Kingdom of God. I knew there would be a great price, but I went forward to the altar for prayer. The power of God was so strong that I fell to the floor.

I received a prophetic word that there was a tremendous anointing on my life for hurting people. Through the prophet, the Lord said that I would go through much emotional pain in order for God to use me to minister healing and deliverance to the abused and hurting. I was asked whether I was willing to pay that price. I said yes. I had already been through so much in my life; I thought that things could not possibly get any worse. But I was wrong. Things got terribly worse.

Later that week, I attended another meeting in the eastern part of the country. At that meeting, I received a similar prophetic word.

It was this-
"There is a tremendous anointing on your life for hurting people. God wants you to know that He loves you with a special love. There've been times in the night when you've cried and cried and wondered if God loved you and where He was. God loves you with a special love. He wanted me to tell you that. He's been with you all the time. He's always been with you. You are gold. You have come from far and you have far to go. God wants you to know that He has never left you or forsaken you. He's always been with you. You have to go through the fire because you have a tremendous anointing on you for hurting people. In order for God to use you like this, you have to go through trials and tribulations. You are gold. You have to go through the fire".

Chapter 25
Back To Williamsville

I returned to Williamsville strengthened and encouraged. The day after I returned, Tiffany invited me to her house. She fired off several questions at me. Did you and Brian fool around....you know...have sex since you came back? What happened in Trinidad? What did your pastor tell you? Do you believe the Lord wants you to leave Williamsville? Where will you go? San Francisco? Trinidad? What is your brother's wife's name? Do you have any cousins in Trinidad?

Innocently, I answered all her questions. But then I noticed that as she questioned me she was angry. She was breathing hard, exhaling loudly through her mouth and shaking her foot angrily. So I asked her why she was asking me all those questions. She said that she simply wanted to know how to pray. It was then that I realized that all her questions stemmed from the deliverance and prayer I received in Trinidad. The Lord then showed me that she was the long haired blonde witch that Sonia saw in the vision. I left her house immediately.

Several things happened after that. I stopped attending the church. Brian was angry with me, but I refused to return to that church. I began attending another one in the area. There were fourteen Christian churches in Williamsville with an average membership of four people! This was due to the heavy presence of witchcraft over the town.

The attacks against me grew worse. Every day at noon, I saw, in the Spirit, the door to the motor home open. A woman walked in and came over to the sofa where I sat. She placed her hands around my neck and choked me. I could barely breathe. Brian sat next to me on the sofa, but he was never attacked.

This continued every day for about a month. I never told Brian, and wondered if he sensed what was happening. I prayed for the Lord to show him because I knew that he would not believe me if I told him. One day he asked, "What is that spirit that enters the house at noon every day?"

The spirit that entered the house was a human spirit. I learned from two former witches that witches astral travel into people's houses and attack them. Astral travel involves commanding your spiritual body to leave your physical body and travel in the astral plane. It is a very dangerous practice and can cause death.

In addition to the spiritual attacks against me, the abuse from Brian worsened. It was clear that Brian inherited his abusive behavior from his father. He was angry at me all the time, and was extremely abusive to me. The abuse was physical, mental, and emotional. He controlled and manipulated me and verbally abused me. During all of this, I was still suffering with excessive monthly bleeding. Sometimes I bled for twenty-one days.

While at a Christian conference we attended in Los Angeles, I became very ill. At the opening service, I was bleeding so heavily that I could not stand up. At the end of the service, I told Brian that I needed to go back to the hotel immediately because my clothing was soaked in blood. He forbade me to leave because he wanted to mingle and meet people. I left anyway.

About an hour later, he came back to our hotel room. He told me that he met a couple we knew who were pastors. They asked him where I was and he told them that I had refused to stay with him after the service! They were very surprised by my behavior. I asked him why he lied, but he just snickered at me. An argument followed. He then picked up a can of coke which he was drinking and threw it all over my clothes that were hanging in the closet. I tried to run out of the room, but as I ran past him, he knocked me down to the floor .

On another occasion, I was standing on a crate in the yard. He wanted to use the crate, but instead of asking me to get off the crate, he pulled it out from under me and I fell to the ground.

I endured the abuse and the spiritual attacks for several months until I felt that I could not cope anymore. I was being severely attacked by demonic spirits, witches and my own husband. Once more, I begged him for us to leave Williamsville and move to another town, but he refused. I told him about what was revealed during my deliverance in Trinidad and what Tiffany did when I returned. I told him that I suspected that she was a witch, but he would not believe me. He was angry with me for accusing his friends of being witches. He treated me with hatred and contempt. He did not support me or protect me, but joined with them in the attack against me. I continued to pray every day for my husband's eyes to be opened to the truth of what was taking place in Williamsville. But I was once more getting weary. In a weakened state, I left again for Trinidad to re-gain my strength.

Chapter 26

More Abuse

I had intended to stay in Trinidad for three weeks and then return to California. But when I tried to return, Brian forbade me to do so until I came back to the church and submitted to the Associate Pastor who was a high priestess. I refused.

I stayed in Trinidad for nine months. While there, my father became ill. He suspected that he had contracted AIDS. We urged him to get tested immediately. But he was afraid to go for the test. So I offered to take him.

The results of the test took a few weeks to be released. During that time, Daddy came over to my brother's house, where I was staying, almost every day to talk. He talked about many things and fearfully contemplated his life. I urged him to repent of his sins and receive Jesus as his Lord and Savior. But he said that there was something horrible that he had done that God would never forgive him for. I knew that he was referring to him sexually abusing me. I assured him that the Lord would forgive him if he would only repent and confess what he did. But his guilt was so great that he could not. The HIV test results came back negative and he was back to his former self.

While I was in Trinidad, Brian told the Associate Pastor, her daughter-in-law Tiffany and everyone in the Church what I told him about their involvement in witchcraft! It caused a major upheaval.

Tiffany refused to allow me to live on their property. She said that Brian was welcome to stay, but I was not! Brian refused to move from Tiffany's. I asked him where I would live when I returned, and he said that he did not know. He stressed that he was going to continue living at Tiffany's.

After nine long months of separation, Brian came to Trinidad to take me back to Williamsville. But there were still the same conditions to my being able to return. I must submit to the Associate Pastor and come back to the church.

Surprisingly, my mother told Brian that she wanted to have a meeting with us. My sister-in-law, Sonia, also attended the meeting. Mummy told Brian that she was afraid for my safety! She was fearful that I might die if I returned to Williamsville. Brian's reply to her was, "So what if she dies? Everybody has to die."

My pastor also requested a meeting with us. At the meeting he counseled Brian on the importance of a husband protecting his wife. He agreed. He finally lifted the criteria under which I could return. However, I had my own conditions under which I would go back to Williamsville. He must go back alone and find us a real house to live in, as well as proper provision. I refused to go back until he did.

About three weeks later, he called to let me know that he

found us a house to rent, and that it was okay for me to return. A few days after, I was on a plane heading back to California. We spent the first two nights in a hotel, because it would take two days before the house was ready to be moved into.

But the day we moved into our new home, Brian revealed some startling information. He would not be moving in with me, but would continue to live at Tiffany's! He had deceived me, and lied to me. I asked him if he would at least stay at nights. But he said no.

There was a lot of demonic activity in the house. At nights I could not sleep because of the eerie disturbances throughout the house. I was terrified. I asked him if he would leave the dog with me at night but he refused.

Each day Brian came by to visit me for an hour, and then left. One day I was under so much spiritual attack that I begged him to stay with me that night. But he cruelly said no. I cried, begged and pleaded, and told him that I was afraid, but he still refused. That night I had one of the worst spiritual attacks that I ever had.

After much prayer and crying out to the Lord to change the situation, Brian finally agreed to move in with me. He had found us another place to rent in the eastern part of town. There was ample room for the motor home, which he parked alongside the house.

Shortly after we moved, Brian got a job in San Francisco. This meant that he would be gone for four to five days each week, and would only be home for a few days. I was now once more alone for several days each week.

Now that Tiffany found out that I knew she was a witch, and also part of the plot to destroy me....... the spiritual attacks against me grew even more intense. The days and nights were bad, but the nights were worse. That's because there is more witchcraft activity at night, especially after 1:00 pm.

It was so scary that I cannot adequately articulate it. I could see and sense the demonic spirits as they manifested in the house. Witches also astral traveled into my home and physically attacked me. They choked me and applied pressure to my chest. I was on the alert day and night for five years.

Throughout the time I lived there, I learned more how to fight spiritually. Sometimes the Lord had me bind the demonic spirits, and other times He had me use the weapon of praise and worship. I had to fight as though my life depended on it......and it did.

In the midst of the intense attacks, the Lord protected and preserved me. At times He would show me the angels that were assigned to protect me. They would manifest in the house, and I saw them through my spiritual eyes.

One night, though, I actually saw them with my natural eyes. That night was a particularly ominous night. The darkness and heaviness in the house was cloying. As usual, I slept fitfully.

I had been asleep for a few hours when I woke up suddenly. The window facing the bed was illuminated with a brilliant light.

Standing outside the house, facing the window, was a huge angel. His garments were a luminous white that was not of this world. His hair was a coppery gold color, and his eyes were bright and gentle. He had a beautiful smile on his face. His sword was drawn and was upraised. His face was turned to the side as he talked with someone else whom I could not see. I fell asleep, but was again awakened. This time I not only saw the same angel, but another one at the other window! This was the person who the first angel was talking to. The Lord showed me that He had placed these angels around the entire house to protect me! I fell asleep, with the wonderful knowledge that my Heavenly Father was with me and protecting me.

Chapter 27

"If You Leave Me You Will Die"

I was very concerned about the spiritual climate in Williamsville. I wanted to start an intercessory group to pray for the town. But every time I found people to pray with me, it turned out to be a disaster. The first two women who promised to pray with me confessed that they were former witches. They shared a lot with me about witchcraft, astral travel and how witches and Satanists operate. One of them, Debbie, told me that Tiffany was indeed a witch. She and Tiffany belonged to different covens. They were rivals. She and Tiffany cast spells over each other. The other woman, Mary, shared that her husband was a Satanist and had a satanic altar in their bedroom.

Debbie and Mary jokingly explained how they frequently astral traveled into each other's homes. They shared how Debbie would be on the phone talking to Mary when suddenly she would astral travel into her home. Debbie would jokingly ask Mary, "What are you doing here in my house while I am talking to you on the phone?"

The prayer meetings with Debbie and Mary were not working out. I felt that they were still joyfully reminiscing about when they were witches. I discerned that they still loved practicing witchcraft. So I stopped praying with them.

The next person I tried to pray with was the wife of our former landlord. She seemed to be a wonderful Christian, but she later confessed that her husband was a warlock. So I stopped praying with her as well. I cried out to God to send me true sold out born-again Christians with whom I could pray. And He did!

He sent me two pastors, a husband and wife, who used to live in another town. The Lord had instructed them to move to Williamsville just after I began praying in earnest for the right prayer partners. In a very short time, we became very close and began interceding for the town and for Brian. We met together and prayed every day from 7:00 am to 1:00 pm or later. Our sessions were powerful and filled with the presence of God. Many prophetic utterances were released during those prayer meetings.

The spiritual attacks continued, but through it the Lord was training me for greater spiritual warfare. My husband grew more abusive, but the Lord was birthing in me a strong anointing to heal the brokenhearted.

The abuse from Brian was horrendous. Although he had a very lucrative salary, he only gave me $20 per week for groceries and other necessities. He also expected that money to be used to provide his meals when he came home from work. I usually ate very meagerly or not at all when he was away at work, but ensured that when he returned home at the weekend he had plenty to eat. My new friends, and prayer partners, later began to provide me with meals while he was at work.

When Brian came home from work, he searched through the garbage to find evidence of what I might have done while he was away. Once I bought two 59 cent hamburgers from Mc Donald's and threw the wrappers in the garbage. He found them and yelled at me because I bought them. He said, "So that's what you've been up to when I was away".

Whenever he was leaving to go back to work in San Francisco, I always had to remind him to give me the twenty dollars for groceries. He never wanted to give it to me and gave it grudgingly when I asked him for it.

On weekends when he came home from work, I always had the house immaculately clean. One night I had a candle lit dinner prepared, with soft music playing. I made a gourmet meal using the few groceries I was able to purchase. The first thing Brian always did when he came home was to hug the dog and roll around on the floor with him. After about 30 minutes of doing this, he would then speak to me. He had told me that he loved the dog more than he loved me. He also said that the dog spoke to him, and insisted that I was not at the spiritual level he was to hear the dog speak!

That night when Brian saw the candle lit dinner and heard the soft music playing, he got angry and yelled, " What is all this nonsense? I don't want all this garbage!" He turned on the lights, blew out the candles and turned off the music. He complained about the meal, and said he did not want any fancy food..........just meat and a baked potato.

Nothing I did or said pleased him. He criticized me all the time. He blamed me for everything. One day I went to the grocery. The sun was shining brightly. It was a brilliant day. But by the time I returned home, the rain began to fall heavily. Brian blamed me for the rain. He told me, "It's your fault. You took the sunshine away. You made it rain."

He spent most of his time in the motor-home. At nights he slept in the bedroom for two hours, tossing and turning restlessly. He said that he could not sleep on the same bed with me. After two hours of restless sleep, he would go into the motor-home to sleep.

One day I observed that he had filled numerous bottles of water and stored them in the cabinet. When I asked him what they were for, he told me that it was for me to use after the rapture. The rapture relates to the return of Jesus Christ as outlined in 1 Thessalonians 4:15-17- "For this we say to you by the word of the Lord, that we who are alive and remain until the coming of the Lord will by no means precede those who are asleep. For the Lord Himself will descend from heaven with a shout, with the voice of an archangel, and with the trumpet of God. And the dead in Christ will rise first. Then we who are alive and remain shall be caught up together with them in the clouds to meet the Lord in the air. And thus we shall always be with the Lord".

The rapture is the carrying away of the Church into heaven when all non-believers will be left behind during the Great

Tribulation period. Brian said that he was going to heaven and I would be left behind on the earth to suffer through the Great Tribulation because I had lost my salvation.

I wanted to get a job so I could have more money to buy food and essentials, but Brian forbade me to work. In any case, it was very difficult to get a job because there was a lot of racism in Williamsville. Because I was black, I was turned down for many jobs. Both Brian and I were the brunt of many racial slurs because people resented the fact that he was white and I was black. Eventually, through prayer, I found a job as a cashier at the department store.

One day, Brian cut the phone wires when I was talking to my sister in Trinidad. He heard me talking to my sister about the abuse, and he did not want my family to know about it. He thought that they would persuade me to leave him. He also had two guns in the house. Once, when I told him I was leaving, he told me that if I left I would die.

I had no transportation, and had to rely on him to take me to the grocery and other places. He did not want me to go anywhere, and I was a virtual prisoner in my home. I prayed and asked God for a car. And I got one!

One day Brian told me he was buying me a car! He bought me an old sports car that did not work properly. The gas gauge did not work, the tires were bad, the engine was faulty, and the turn signals did not work. But it got me to where I needed to go. He also bought himself another car which he repaired and fixed up beautifully. But he refused to have any repairs done to my car.

He did not want me to drive my car anywhere except to work and to the grocery store. But while he was at work, I drove into the neighboring towns. One day he cut the wires in the car engine so that I could not go anywhere.

Chapter 28

Escape

I descended into a place of great weariness. I was tired of the intense spiritual warfare and I was tired of Brian's abuse. I was tired of praying for him to be delivered and seeing no results. I came to realize the magnitude of the spiritual bondage he was in.

One day a friend of Brian's, a young woman named Gail, told me that she needed deliverance. I invited her to our home to minister to her. She wanted to wait until Brian came home from work, so that he could help with the deliverance. When he came home, Brian said that he wanted to pray and ask God if he should be part of the deliverance. He went out to the motor home to pray. On his return he said, "God told me that I cannot minister deliverance to Gail because Satan cannot cast our Satan!"

I grew numb with fear at those words. I realized then that I had to leave. But I did not know how. I had no money and had nowhere to go. I tried to leave before, but got as far as the county line, when I had to come back home because I had no place to go. When I returned home, he laughed mockingly at me.

Like so many abusers, there is a cycle of abuse and remorse. Brian would abuse me and then would cry and say that he was sorry. Abusive husbands appeal to the innate compassion in women. Many women feel compassion for their abusive mates when they appear remorseful, and they end up remaining in the abusive marriage. Added to that, the abuser exercises so much control over their victim that it is hard for them to break free from the bondage. On many occasions, I felt so much compassion for Brian that I decided to stay and try to fix him. But I could not.

A series of events catapulted me into making the decision to leave. For years he tormented me with accusing his friends of being witches. These friends were witches who had infiltrated the church and were masquerading as Christians. I had prayed daily for Brian's eyes to be opened to the truth. But it never happened.

These witches decided to launch an all-out attack against me. I found out later that Brian was the one who initiated the attack. He met with some of them and told them that he was tired of my disobedience to him and asked them to "pray" for me.

That night I could not sleep. There was a cacophony of voices ringing in my head. Hundreds of voices spoke into my mind at the same time about mundane things. They chanted for hours and hours, and I could not stop it. The effect was torturous.

At the same time, these witches projected the most horrible images of my death into my mind. My heart beat erratically and I felt that I was going insane. I jumped up off the bed and began to run to my car to drive away. I did not know where to go, but I knew that I had to get out of there. But the Lord stopped me before I could leave. I would have walked into a trap that would have resulted in my death. I cried out to God and the attack ceased.

The next day, my brother called me from Trinidad. He told me to get out before my husband killed me. His phone call was the catalyst that brought about my escape. A few days later I received a large sum of money that was owed to me from my previous job in Trinidad. I formulated a plan of escape. I secretly opened a bank account. I called my cousin Diana in Maryland and discussed my situation with her. She told me that I could stay with them.

In secret, I began to ship my books and other personal items to Maryland. I became very ill during this process. I had become even more physically weakened by the excessive loss of blood each month. I visited a doctor in another town, and she told me that the fibroids had grown back fully. I had to have a hysterectomy immediately.

Brian was at work in San Francisco so I called him on his cell phone. He had always refused to give me his cell phone number, but I located his cell phone bill and found the number.

When I told him about the surgery, he was angry that I called him. I needed his approval for the surgery because I would have to use his health insurance coverage. He finally consented, and I called back the doctor to set up the surgery for the next week. I would need to have a blood transfusion before the surgery because my hemoglobin count was precariously low.

Brian came home a few days later. I was scheduled to have the blood transfusion the same day he came home. As I discussed the surgery and the blood transfusion with him, he said "I never gave you permission to go ahead with the surgery". I reminded him of my phone call, but he was adamant and said that he was not paying for the surgery.

The co-payment for the surgery was only five hundred dollars! I told him that my condition was life threatening and that without the surgery I would die. But he would not budge.
He walked out of the house angrily and went into the motor home. I began to pray and intercede for God to intervene.

About a half hour later I went to the motor home to speak to him again about the urgency of me having the blood transfusion that day and the surgery a couple days later. Brian had drawn something on a piece of paper. He thrust it angrily at me and said, "What is that?" The drawing looked like a pot with a lid on it, and I told him so. With a glazed vacant look in his eyes, he said "That's a coffin…….. your coffin! You are going to die in the operating room". Fear washed over me instantly.

Brian finally consented to me having the blood transfusion and the surgery. I asked him to drive me to the hospital, which was in another town about one hour's drive away, but he refused. So I got in my car, and with tears streaming down my face, I drove myself to the hospital.

The blood transfusion was supposed to last about two hours, but when I got to the hospital I was told that I would need a lot of blood and would have to stay overnight. The head nurse on the ward was a wonderful Christian woman. I asked her to call my husband to let him know that I had to stay in the hospital overnight. But he deliberately refused to pick up the phone so all the calls went to the answering machine. The nurse left several messages for him to call the hospital, but he never did. That nurse was so compassionate to me. She could not understand how a husband could do that to his wife.

My wonderful Heavenly Father orchestrated it so that all the nurses on the ward that night were Christians. The head nurse gathered them all into my room where they prayed for me! The presence of God descended in that room that night.

I returned home the next day to a surly angry Brian. He was very hostile to me for several days. I had the hysterectomy a few days later.

Going into the surgery, a spirit of fear attacked me. Brian's statement that I was going to die in the operating room tormented me. After the surgery, a dear Christian friend who lived in another town, and whom I had recently met, took me into her home where she cared for me for two weeks after the surgery. I was in a lot of pain and unable to do very much for eight weeks. But when I returned to my house, Brian insisted that I do the housework. He wanted me to sit on a chair next to the stove and cook. I refused.

All the abuse, the spiritual attacks from demons and witches and the hysterectomy had worn me out. I became physically, mentally and emotionally weary. I lay on the sofa for several weeks wanting to die. I asked God for the strength to leave as I planned. I secretly bought my plane ticket and continued to execute my plan of escape.

A few weeks after the surgery, when Brian was at work, I left. A few days before I escaped, he came home from work as usual. He stayed for four days and then headed back to San Francisco. He did not suspect what I was about to do. The moment he left, I started to pack.

I was so drained, stressed out and confused that it took me over eight hours to pack two suitcases. I cried all the time. I would put a few clothes into the suitcase, and then had to stop to rest because I felt so exhausted and distressed. This cycle continued for hours.

Suddenly I heard someone drive into the garage. It was Lorraine, a woman who I previously worked with at the department store. She told me, "You just lie down and relax; I am going to take care of everything for you". She took over the packing. She spoke to me all through it. She encouraged me. She said, "You are going to be okay. You are doing the right thing. God is with you. Do not worry. You are going to make it" She was such a blessing sent by God to help me leave.

I wrote Brian a note telling him that I was leaving. I did not tell him where I was moving to. For my safety and protection that information had to be kept secret. I left my wedding ring on the table. I took the dog to the kennel where Brian could pick him up when he came home.

Chapter 29
Learning to Live, Laugh and Love Myself

I arrived in Maryland, bruised and battered. As I unpacked my suitcases, there were several notes from Lorraine tucked away among my belongings. She had written words of encouragement on each note!

My cousin Diana and her husband David took me into their home and helped me tremendously. They gave me a job in the company they owned and were very supportive to me.

I was a broken down shattered mess. I had to re-learn how to talk, act, and dress. There was so much that was stolen from me……….especially my identity. I did not know who I was anymore. I just wanted to withdraw from everyone and everything. Added to that, I was now dealing with menopause because the hysterectomy had plunged me into surgical menopause.

Two weeks after I moved to Maryland I experienced a horrible spiritual attack. I lay exhausted in my bedroom when suddenly I had trouble breathing. I walked downstairs searching for my cousin to help me. As I walked down the steps, I felt the breath leaving my body. I collapsed on the floor and my body pulsated violently. My breathing grew more and more shallow as I fought for air. I was dying. My cousins came running over to me and surrounded me. They prayed and bound the demonic spirits that were attacking me, and I began to breathe normally again.

God began the process of restoring everything that I had lost. The process was hard. But God did a great restorative work in my life. However, I no longer wanted to be in ministry. I just wanted to be a "regular" Christian who sat in the back of the Church and did nothing. But God would not let me go. I sent out many job applications, confident that I would get a great job in my field. But that did not happen. I got a mediocre job that paid just enough to take care of my needs. Everything pointed to the fact that the Lord wanted me to be in ministry full time.

A few months after I moved to Maryland I called Brian to tell him that I forgave him. He cried and told me that he was sorry for what he did. But that did not influence me as I knew the deceptive cycle of the abuser ……..a cycle of abuse and remorse. He still did not know where I was, and to my knowledge he still does not know to this day. I found out that he waited an entire month after I left before trying to find me. He then reported me missing to the police.

Over the next couple years I began to experience the Lord in greater ways than I could have ever imagined possible. I rushed home to my new apartment from work each day, eager to spend time with the Lord. I would eat hurriedly, take a shower and spend almost all night in the presence of the Lord. I studied the Bible, prayed and worshipped the Lord for hours. The intimacy I developed with Him was so beautiful. He visited me and spoke with me……..and gave me direction for my life. I fell more in love with my Heavenly Father and experienced true love.

I had, and still have, so many glorious experiences with the Lord. One day, as I was lying in my bed worshipping the Lord, He came and took me by the hand and I began to fly with Him across the earth. I was still lying on my bed, but my spirit was flying in the skies with the Lord! At first I was scared, but the Lord, as He held my hand, said, "Do not be afraid."

As we flew across the earth, the Lord showed me the nations of the world He was calling me to minister in. On each nation we flew over, the word 'Lives" were inscribed on them. My heavenly Daddy revealed that He would use me to transform people's lives in those nations.

I then saw a long parade of people pass in front of me. These people all wore their native garments. Many countries were represented………most of which were countries where there were major satanic strongholds, and where people had never heard the gospel. We then began to fly straight up into heaven. All along the way, there were angels sitting on the clouds greeting me and cheering as we flew past.

The Lord also revealed to me that he had called me to be not only a prophet, but an apostle and a pastor. The call is also to severely abused and brokenhearted women and children. He also called me to tear down satanic strongholds, and set the captives free. He revealed other things that he was calling me to do in the Kingdom of God.

The Lord delivered me from the brutal effects of the abortion I had which had troubled me for years. He told me to tell Him to ask my son in heaven to forgive me for what I did. I did. And I was set free.

Shortly after that, I became ordained and started a church in Maryland. A couple years after the church began, the Lord told me to go to Trinidad to resolve the problems with my parents. For years I had tried to talk with them about our problems and how their abuse and rejection had affected me. I had always told them that I loved them and wanted to have a real relationship with them. But they would not listen.

This time, the Lord told me that I was not to tell them the same thing. He instructed me to tell them that I loved them and honored them as my parents, and ask them to forgive me if I had done or said anything to hurt them.

When I arrived in Trinidad, I invited my parents out for breakfast where I planned to talk to them. My father consented, but my mother refused to go. She told Sonia, "I am not going anywhere with her and Harold!" In her mind, I was still "the other woman". For years my siblings and I had encouraged our mother to go for healing and deliverance, but she stubbornly refused. She insisted that there was absolutely nothing wrong with her.

I went to my brother's house to talk to my mother. I asked her why she did not want to go out to breakfast with me and my father. I told her how much I wanted her to come, but she became very angry and violent with me. She yelled at me and threw me down on the floor. Eventually, through much prayer, she consented.

At the breakfast, I told Mummy and Daddy that I loved them and honored them as my parents, and I asked them to forgive me for anything I ever said and did to hurt them. My father wept, but my mother looked at me with hostility.

I also talked to them about blessings and curses, and how biblically, the Jews pronounced blessings over their children........and how those blessings came to pass. I told them that I was concerned about the word curses they had spoken over me and my siblings, and asked them if they would now begin to practice speaking blessings over us. My father agreed, but my mother refused. I had written out some blessings to get them started. Daddy took the list I wrote, and told me afterwards that he read those blessings over us daily.

Chapter 30
Death, Death and More Death

Mummy died a few years later. She had been suffering with Alzheimer's disease. As with Alzheimer's disease, the symptoms developed slowly causing Mummy to forget who she was and where she lived. As time passed, the disease became severe enough to impede her daily tasks. She would turn on all the burners on the gas stove and leave them on for hours and hours. She would make a sandwich by placing a block of soap between two slices of bread. My mother lived with my sister during this painful period. As was customary, my mother was home alone while my sister went to work each day. Over time, it became unsafe for my mother to continue to be in the house by herself. We, my sister, my brother and I, had to make the most difficult decision to place her in a Senior Citizens home. When my siblings visited her at the home, she was disoriented. She often thought she was a young woman still married to my father. I would call her from the United States but she did not know who I was.

I later decided to travel to Trinidad to visit her at the Senior Citizens home. As my sister drove me there, I had so many mixed emotions…….nervousness, apprehension, fear, sorrow and hope. The moment I saw Mummy, I began to cry. There standing before me was a woman who was exhibiting a whole gamut of strange behaviors. She behaved like a child. Then she acted like a teenager. She began to dance, laugh, sing and cry. The worst was when my own mother, Yvonne Harris, did not recognize me. We kept asking her if she knew who I was and she said repeatedly "Yes. You are Yvonne". I began to weep more because it was so difficult to see Mummy in this strange place.....mentally and emotionally....as well as to be now living in that cold, sterile Senior Citizens home.

At the end of my two week visit to Trinidad, I returned to the United States and continued in ministry as a pastor. A couple years after my return, I received a phone call from my sister informing me that my mother had died. Again, I returned to Trinidad. But this time it was to attend my mother's funeral. As I stood at the open casket at the funeral service, I wept for the mother that I never had a close relationship with. I never really knew her as my mother...........but as a combative stranger who fought with me.

Mummy was cremated at the St. James crematorium and her ashes were placed in an urn. So strange, I thought, that this woman with whom I had a volatile relationship could be reduced to mere ashes. My consolation was that she is in heaven with Jesus, because she was a born again Christian.

Three months after my mother's death, I received another telephone call from Trinidad. This time it was from my niece.

My father was dead! In December, my father fell and broke his hip, and was unable to walk. My sister drove him to the hospital where he was told that he would have to undergo surgery. However, he was told by the hospital that they do not do surgeries over the Christmas holidays! He would have to return in January. Daddy suffered terribly for the next month. He was in excruciating pain and he could not walk.

On the appointed day in January when he was scheduled to go back to the hospital, the ambulance came to his home to transport him there. As he was getting ready to leave, my sister felt strongly that she should try one more time to lead him to the Lord. She asked him, "Daddy, would you like to give your life to Jesus Christ?" Daddy's reply was a powerful and emotional "Yes!" My sister led him in a simple prayer of repentance and surrender of his life to Christ. Praise God. Daddy had finally received Jesus Christ as his Lord and personal Savior. An hour later, at the hospital, my father passed away. He is now in heaven with Jesus.

Once again, I was back in Trinidad for another funeral. Daddy was also cremated, and his ashes were placed in an urn. My brother kept both my mother's and father's urns in his living room for several years and refused to dispose of their ashes. Each time we told him that it was time that we disposed of their ashes, he would cry because he was emotionally unable to part with the only remaining vestiges of our parents' lives.

In the same year of my father's death, which was three months after my mother died, my aunt and my uncles all died. My siblings and I now had no parents, aunts and uncles left on both sides of our family. My father's brothers, Clyde and Earl were dead. My mother's siblings, Ernil, Norbert, Lester and Elaine were all dead. My siblings, along with our cousins, concluded that we needed to draw closer to each other. We were now the "older generation" in the family and wanted to leave a greater legacy for the younger ones-a legacy of love, respect, integrity and community. My siblings and I began to develop a real relationship, or what I call a *REAL*ationship, with each other. It was not always easy to do so because of our faulty foundations, but we strived and persevered. We gathered for a special day of prayer and fast where we repented for the sins in our blood line going back to all generations on both sides of the family, and we broke all the generational curses off the family.

Chapter 31

The Barren Now "Sings"

I finally understood why the Lord gave me that scripture in Isaiah 54: 1-6 when I was a very young woman-

> *1"Sing, O barren, you who have not borne! Break forth into singing, and cry aloud, you who have not labored with child! For more are the children of the desolate than the children of the married woman," says the LORD. 2"Enlarge the place of your tent, and let them stretch out the curtains of your dwellings; Do not spare; Lengthen your cords, And strengthen your stakes. 3 For you shall expand to the right and to the left, And your descendants will inherit the nations, And make the desolate cities inhabited. 4 "Do not fear, for you will not be ashamed; Neither be disgraced, for you will not be put to shame; For you will forget the shame of your youth, And will not remember the reproach of your widowhood anymore. 5 For your Maker is your husband, The LORD of hosts is His name; And your Redeemer is the Holy One of Israel; He is called the God of the whole earth. 6 For the LORD has called you Like a woman forsaken and grieved in spirit, Like a youthful wife when you were refused," Says your God.*

Verse One

[1]"Sing, O barren, you who have not borne! Break forth into singing, and cry aloud, you who have not labored with child! For more are the children of the desolate than the children of the married woman," says the LORD.

I was barren, both mentally and emotionally– unproductive, without capacity to interest or attract, unloved, unfruitful, desolate, bereft, abandoned and rejected by men and women. I was physically barren -unable to conceive and bear any children, childless, and without progeny or successors. But I found the love of my life, the one who loves me unconditionally, the Lord God Almighty- The Father, His son Jesus Christ, my Lord and Savior, and the Holy Spirit, my comforter. I have an intimate relationship with Him that is filled with love, joy and peace. And it is because of Him and Who He is that I can "sing." "Sing" does not mean to literally sing. It means: to rejoice, to be happy, to be glad.......in spite of your situation and circumstances. I can rejoice, be happy and glad because I am experiencing the love of God. I am no longer unproductive, unloved, unfruitful, desolate, bereft, abandoned and rejected. I no longer look to men to fill the void in my life. No longer am I looking for love "in all the wrong places". I love myself and I know that I am valuable and worthy.

The journey I took to get to this place was long and arduous. I've made a lot of mistakes……and learned from them. I have faced obstacles that seemed insurmountable. I have had seasons of loving myself and then hating myself when I did anything wrong or that did not measure up to people's expectations of me. I was hard on myself when I messed up, and still dealt with rejection and self-rejection. But God has helped me to not "stay down" when I felt defeated or failed at something, but to rise up, learn from my mistakes and keep moving forward.

One of the things that I struggled with was being alone over the holidays. Christmas, New Years, Thanksgiving and Valentine's day were the worse times for me. For many years, I cried during those holidays, especially on the nights of Christmas Eve and New Year's. I could not decorate my home for Christmas because it reminded me of what I did not have, and longed for, to be a part of a loving healthy family. It took several years for me to overcome this. Normally, on Thanksgiving I would be alone at home eating leftovers or a non-traditional Thanksgiving dinner. One year, for the first time at Thanksgiving, I cooked a great meal, stayed at home by myself and celebrated Thanksgiving with the Lord. I thanked Him for everything that He has done for me- things that I know of and things I would only know about when I get to heaven. I thanked Him for who He is to me. It was the best thanksgiving I ever had. That year also, at Christmas, I decorated my home, played Christmas music and had the happiest Christmas that I've ever had. I basked in the loving presence of the Lord.

I am childless and unable to have any children naturally due to the hysterectomy I had several years ago. But I have been blessed to have many spiritual sons and daughters in several nations. They all call me "Mom" "Ma" or "Mother".

<u>Verses 2 & 3</u>

2 "Enlarge the place of your tent, and let them stretch out the curtains of your dwellings; Do not spare; Lengthen your cords, And strengthen your stakes. 3 For you shall expand to the right and to the left, And your descendants will inherit the nations, And make the desolate cities inhabited.

God wants us to be prosperous. When people hear the word "prosper", they think only of wealth. But the word "prosper" means much more than that. In the Bible, in 3 John 1:2 it says- Beloved, I pray that you may prosper in all things and be in health, just as your soul prospers. To prosper means to succeed, to bloom, to grow and increase. God wants us prosper in every area of our lives. He wants us to be whole and healthy and to succeed I everything we do. For God to prosper us, we have to let go of the old and the familiar and prepare to receive the new and unfamiliar. We have to agree with God to let go of our pain, suffering and disappointments. We have to trust Him and the persons He has sent to bring healing and deliverance to us. I had to do this. It did not happen all at once. It was a process. I first had to get to know God intimately- His nature and His character. And once I discovered that God truly loves me and wants the best for me, I was able to trust Him. And then I was able to prosper.

God has taken me from seasons of heartache, depression, trauma and barrenness to seasons of peace and prosperity. He has blessed me in every area of my life. In 2005, God told me to leave my job and go into ministry full-time. I had already been pastoring a Church in Maryland, while working a secular job. But now He wanted me to give up that job and enter into full time ministry with no salary, and depend on Him to supply all my needs. It took me awhile to obey Him because the thought of having no regular monthly salary was frightening, but I eventually followed His directions. The Lord has supernaturally provided for me since that time. Whenever I needed money, He would direct people to give me a financial gift. I never asked anyone for money. God simply instructed them and they obeyed. There were many occasions when different people would come to my home the day before my rent was due, hand me an envelope with money, and say "God told me to give you this". It was usually the exact amount of money I needed for my rent!

We have to learn from our painful experiences and not become bitter but better. Our experiences can help someone else who has been through the same things we have been. I now have the privilege of ministering healing and deliverance to abused and brokenhearted women and children. I am also serving God in the areas of training, equipping and ordaining Christians for ministry, and preaching the Word of God. I lead missions to third world countries, such as Haiti, to empower abused and displaced women, children and men, provide training in the areas of hygiene, nutrition and life skills, as well as to supply food, toiletries, clothing and other essential supplies to impoverished men, women and children.

Verse 4

4 "Do not fear, for you will not be ashamed; Neither be disgraced, for you will not be put to shame; For you will forget the shame of your youth, And will not remember the reproach of your widowhood anymore.

God wants to take away all your fears and shame. Fear is a crippling emotion caused by the belief that someone or something is going to harm us or cause us pain. It is a feeling of agitation and anxiety caused by the presence or imminence of danger. There are rational fears and irrational fears. Rational fears act as a catalyst to warn us of impending danger. For example, you can be in an environment or in the presence of a person or persons and become fearful because you sense something evil is about to happen. In this case, rational fear can save you from a dangerous person or situation. Irrational fear, however, is not based on anything tangible. It is an abiding feeling of dread that someone is going to hurt you or something bad is going to happen to you. It could be fear of being hurt again, fear of dying, fear of failure, fear of success, fear of intimacy, fear of man, fear of rejection, or fear of the unknown.

I know this first hand. I used to be afraid of everything and everyone. I felt that everyone was going to hurt me and reject me. I was afraid of saying the wrong thing and doing the wrong thing. I put up walls to protect my emotions. But as I began to experience the love of God, those fears diminished. In the Bible, in 1 John 4:18, it says: "There is no fear in love; but perfect love casts out fear, because fear involves torment. But he who fears has not been made perfect in love". Fear cripples you, immobilizes you and torments you and keeps you from fulfilling your divine destiny. Where there is perfect love, there is no fear. God's perfect love for us gives us boldness, confidence, security and protection. You conquer fear with love.

Fear is also a spirit. I had to be delivered from a spirit of fear. The first spirit the enemy usually sends to you is the spirit of fear. If the enemy can make you afraid of him then he's got you under his control and will attack you in other areas of your life. The Lord does not want you to be afraid anymore. He wants you to let Him love you unconditionally, the way you have never been loved before. As you allow God to take control of your life (He does a better job than us of controlling our own lives), you will not be disgraced or put to shame. You will forget the shame associated with the abuse and other painful experiences you have been through. The word widowhood in this verse means "a desolate place". You will not be desolate anymore. Nor will you be disappointed as you put your trust in God.

<u>Verses 5 &6</u>

5 For your Maker is your husband, The Lord of hosts is His name; And your Redeemer is the Holy One of Israel; He is called the God of the whole earth. 6 For the Lord has called you Like a woman forsaken and grieved in spirit, Like a youthful wife when you were refused," Says your God.

God is calling you to come to Him as you are. Come with your grief. Come with your sins. Come with your drug or alcohol addiction. Come with your anger. Come with your hatred. Come with your criminal background. Come with all your "mess". He will not reject you. Surrender your life to him and receive his Son Jesus Christ as your Lord and personal Savior. He will transform your life. It will not happen overnight. It is a lifelong process. If you do not know how to receive Him as your Lord and personal Savior, there is a salvation prayer at the end of this book that you can pray.

Maybe, you have received Jesus Christ as your Lord and Savior, but you have been abused, abandoned and rejected. You don't love yourself and have thought of killing yourself. You find that your life has no purpose. God, your maker, wants to heal you and deliver you and cause you to prosper in every area of your life. Talk to Him. Be real with Him. Tell Him everything-your pain, disappointments and fears. Ask Him to heal and deliver you. He will! And He may send someone who has been through what you have been to minister healing and deliverance to you. I pray that you will find joy, peace and prosperity as I have. I am so thankful to God for allowing me to experience all that I have so that I can be used effectively in His kingdom. One the most rewarding things that I enjoy, is to counsel and empower women and children who are victims of sexual, physical and emotional abuse and domestic violence. The Lord has given me the precious gift to feel people's emotional pain, so I can effectively minister healing to them. Out of the barrenness in my life has come joy, peace and fulfillment. Now I can sing. I rejoice in the Lord. I shout for joy. There are still trials. There are still tribulations. But, the barren has learned to "sing".

Salvation Prayer

Dear Lord, I come to you just as I am with all my emotional baggage. I believe that your Son, Jesus Christ, to die on the cross for my sins. I believe that Jesus Christ is the way, the truth, and the life, and that no one comes to the Father except through Him. I believe that God has raised Jesus from the dead. I repent of my sins and invite Jesus to come into my life and make me a born-again child of God. From this day forward, I will live for you, and allow you to take complete control of my life, in Jesus Name. Amen.

About The Author

Lisa has 30 years of experience in counselling and liberating abused and battered women, children and men from every stratum of society. She has a tremendous compassion for abused, hurting and abandoned women and children, a powerful anointing to heal the brokenhearted, and the mentally and physically sick, and to deliver those oppressed with demonic spirits. She has ministered deliverance and healing, both emotional and physical, to hundreds of marginalized, impoverished, sexually, physically, mentally and emotionally abused women and children in many nations. Many of them have gone on to become productive men and women. Some have become ministers of the gospel, teachers, authors, and entrepreneurs, and one a politician. Lisa has also counseled and rehabilitated prisoners and juvenile offenders in jails, prisons and juvenile centers.

Her radio program, Restoring The Foundations, which for four years aired on the Christian Radio Network, Isaac 98.1 FM in Trinidad and Tobago was broadcast globally to audiences as far as China. Lisa's program presented dynamic, divine revelation for restoring godly foundations in families, communities, churches and nations.

Lisa, an apostle, prophet, Christian educator and preacher, has served the Lord as Youth Minister, Children's Church Director, Director of Audio/Visual Ministries and Director of the Christian Education Board of The Fellowship Center in Florida, co-pastor of Damascus Road Ministries, California, founder and senior pastor of the Shepherd's Heart Ministries USA, and Glory Tabernacle Worship Center Trinidad and Tobago. She is also the founder of Releasing His Glory Ministries USA, The Glory School USA and Trinidad and Tobago, Broken But Not Destroyed- a ministry to abused and broken women and children, Kingdom Advance Operations, and Lisa Harris Ministries in Central Florida. Lisa trains, equips and release believers into their ministries and other destinies. She travels to the nations to preach, teach, minister healing and deliverance, and build and strengthen Churches and ministries.

Lisa also has a Bachelor of Arts Degree with honors in Psychology and Communications from the City University of New York, and a Master's Degree with honors in International Relations and Conflict Resolution from American Public University. In her Master's Degree program, Lisa has also studied Sexual Exploitation of Children and Criminal Profiling.

If you would like to contact Apostle Lisa Harris-Corbitt
to minister or speak at an event,
please email her at lacorbitt@gmail.com
or visit her website at www.lisaharriministries.com

www.ingramcontent.com/pod-product-compliance
Lightning Source LLC
Chambersburg PA
CBHW050635300426
44112CB00012B/1810